Praise for *Macbeth*

'A clever, heartfelt and, in the br⏤   ⏤⏤ ⏤⏤⏤ persuasive
sense, feminist revisiting of Shakespeare's great tragedy. Bold,
innovative and bleakly comic, it justifies itself gloriously.'
Daily Telegraph

'Wry, haunting . . . a witty, disconcerting exploration of
Lady Macbeth's role in this story and, eventually, a
commentary on the representation of women in drama
generally . . . [There is a] delicate balance of wit and horror
in the script.' *The Times*

'Harris's stunning vision evolves into a response to
Shakespeare with the power to challenge this greatest of
classics on almost equal terms.' *The Scotsman*

'There are moments in Zinnie Harris's new play where the
sense of a back-and-forth between the past and the present is
so delicious that it's mouth-watering . . . The chief delight is
in the clever script . . . It's exhilarating to watch a dramatist
who's so confident with her material.' *What's On Stage*

'Audacious . . . sometimes witty, always intelligent.'
Guardian

'Writer and director Zinnie Harris has made one of her
stocks-in-trade the reimagining of well-known plays to
accentuate the female narratives at their heart. They all feel as
though they've been building to this . . . The stark clarity of
Harris's text [is] masterfully traditional and refreshingly new.'
The Stage

'A thrilling reimagining that lays bare the real power behind
the blood-spattered throne.' *Herald*

Macbeth (an undoing)

Zinnie Harris's plays include the multi-award-winning
Further than the Furthest Thing (National Theatre/Tron
Theatre; winner of the 1999 Peggy Ramsay Award, 2001
John Whiting Award, Edinburgh Fringe First Award), *How
to Hold Your Breath* (Royal Court Theatre; joint winner of
the Berwin Lee Award), *The Wheel* (National Theatre of
Scotland; joint winner of the 2011 Amnesty International
Freedom of Expression Award, Fringe First Award),
Nightingale and Chase (Royal Court Theatre), *Midwinter*,
Solstice (both RSC), *Fall* (Traverse Theatre/RSC), *By Many
Wounds* (Hampstead Theatre), the trilogy *This Restless
House*, based on Aeschylus' *Oresteia* (Citizens
Theatre/National Theatre of Scotland; Best New Play, Critics
Award for Theatre in Scotland) and *Meet Me at Dawn*
(Traverse Theatre). She has also adapted Ibsen's *A Doll's
House* for the Donmar Warehouse, Strindberg's *Miss Julie* for
the National Theatre of Scotland, *(the fall of) The Master
Builder* for Leeds Playhouse, and *The Duchess (of Malfi)* for
the Royal Lyceum Theatre, Edinburgh. She received an Arts
Foundation Fellowship for playwriting, and was Writer in
Residence at the RSC, 2000–2001. She is the Professor of
Playwriting and Screenwriting at the University of St
Andrews and the Associate Artistic Director at the Royal
Lyceum Theatre in Edinburgh.

ZINNIE HARRIS

Macbeth (an undoing)

after
SHAKESPEARE

with an afterword by
DAN REBELLATO

faber

First published in 2023
by Faber and Faber Limited
The Bindery, 51 Hatton Garden
London, EC1N 8HN

Published in this edition in 2024

Typeset by Brighton Gray
Printed and bound in the UK by CPI Group (Ltd), Croydon CRO 4YY

A CIP record for this book
is available from the British Library

ISBN 978-0-571-39097-7

Printed and bound in the UK on FSC® certified paper in line with our continuing
commitment to ethical business practices, sustainability and the environment.
For further information see faber.co.uk/environmental-policy

2 4 6 8 10 9 7 5 3 1

Macbeth (an undoing) was first performed at the Royal Lyceum Theatre Edinburgh on 4 February 2023, with the following cast, in alphabetical order:

Macbeth Adam Best
Lady Macbeth Nicole Cooper
Carlin Liz Kettle
Duncan / Murderer 3 / Courtier Marc Mackinnon
Bloody Soldier / Lennox Taqi Nazeer
Lady Macduff Jade Ogugua
Missy / Malcolm Star Penders
Banquo James Robinson
Ross / Murderer 1 Laurie Scott
Macduff / Doctor / Courtier 1 Paul Tinto
Mae Farrah Anderson Fryer, Matilde Sabino Hunt,
    Bella Svaasand
Serving Boy / Murderer 2 Frankie Bunker, Charlie Corliss

Writer/Director Zinnie Harris
Set Designer Tom Piper
Costume Designer & Associate Set Designer Alex Berry
Lighting Designer Lizzie Powell
Composer Oğuz Kaplangı
Sound Designer Pippa Murphy
Movement Director Emily Jane Boyle
Fight & Intimacy Director Kaitlin Howard
Dramaturg Frances Poet
Casting Director Simone Pereira Hind CDG and
    Anna Dawson
Assistant Director Nerida Bradley

Macbeth (an undoing) toured to the Rose Theatre, Kingston, on 8 March 2024, and to the Theatre for a New Audience at Polonsky Shakespeare Center, New York, on 5 April 2024. It returned to the Royal Lyceum, Edinburgh, on 14 May 2024. The production involved the following changes:

Lady Macduff / Mae Emmanuella Cole
Macduff / Doctor Thierry Mabonga

Production Manager Niall Black
Producer Hannah Roberts

Characters

Carlin

Missy

Mae

Bloody Soldier

Macbeth

Banquo

Ross

Lady Macbeth

Duncan

Lady Macduff

Malcolm

Lennox

Macduff

Doctor

Murderer 1

Murderer 2

The play can be performed with a cast of ten actors.

MACBETH (AN UNDOING)

Act One

ONE

Darkness.

A woman steps out into the light and looks at the audience. The stage is bare.

Carlin
Knock knock knock.
Who's there?

She looks again out across the stalls, more intent this time.

Misery seekers – here they come. Eyes all nasty and randy for gore. You recognise yourself? Mouths open, tongues out. You're all the same. Death is what you want – blood, despair, the fall of man? It'll be as you last saw it – but no matter, things fare better when they are played and played again. Never an end to your asking for more.
But – what more do we have for your ghouls? Bare boards. Nothing much. If you're looking for pyrotechnics, you'll be disappointed – no thunder to speak of, no heath – no lightning, no rain – what will you do?
No matter you say – blood cold and unmoving – just give us the play!
The play, the play, of course we're here to do the play.

She sniffs, looks around.

Still –
Bit of the highlands painted on a cloth behind might have been nice. Dab of heather, wee bit of gorse –
We were lucky in one place, we got a mat – cushions for the knees as we writhed. In another we were strung from the rafters – fire in our hair.
Not many rafters in this place – more like rain from the roof –

3

She looks up to the roof, puts her hand out.

You can tell the health of a theatre by what fills the stage.

She looks about.

I have a chair.

Beat.

Knock knock knock.
Anyone there?
Oh and there's an assistant – or the assistant to the
assistant – the one newest to the game – and at the back,
script in hand and even now waving me to get off, this is not
the way it should begin, because this story will be told the
way it has always been told. What else use is it otherwise?
The hags on the heath. The woman who went mad. The
man who became a tyrant. Aye sir. Of course – words and
syllables and words and words and hours dreadful, things
strange and the next night the same again . . .

She looks at the audience.

She bends down, knocks on the floor.

Knock knock knock.
Alright, blood-sucking vermin. You'll get what you paid
for!
No merry ending for you.
No dance, no soft turn.
Fog. Mist. Damp like nowhere but in Scotland. A heath.
Winter in May. Snow in June. And a man. Wounded,
dripping with blood –

The light is waiting for the soldier, he walks into it.

Doubtful.
Doubtful.
Doubtful it stood.

The soldier spits.

And the man who says these words – chest caved in,
arrow-head in his thigh, face lacerated – but still he spits
out what he must –
Doubtful.
Doubtful.

The man tries to speak.

Wipes his face of blood.

He takes a breath –

Bloody Soldier
Doubtful.
Doubtful it stood –

The woman breathes out like she has been holding her breath.

Carlin
As two spent swimmers, that do cling together and choke
their art. The merciless Macdonald from the Western Isles –

The soldier looks at the woman.

Bloody Soldier
These are my words.

Carlin
Then say them – sirrah.

The soldier looks at the audience. Stops.

Tries to get his head around the pain. Spits again.

Bloody Soldier
Doubtful it stood, as two spent swimmers that do cling
together and choke their art. But all's too weak for brave
Macbeth – well he deserves that name, with his
brandished steel which smoked.

The woman gets a picnic chair and sits on it.

He looks at her.

Carlin

Go on, go on –

He continues.

Bloody Soldier

With bloody execution carved out his passage – till he faced the slave – and unseamed him from the nave to the chops and fixed his head –

Carlin

It's good, it's good, keep going –

The soldier pauses for a second.

Don't let me put you off.
I'm only a hag, an old woman, vermin to you.

Bloody Soldier

It's a message for the king.

Carlin

Oh the king, well, when we see him.
Here on the heath wandering around.

She knocks on the floor.

Two other women come on to the stage and look at the soldier.

Missy is in her middle years, Mae not much more than a girl.

Bloody Soldier

No sooner had we won than a Norwegian lord saw an advantage and began a fresh assault, and then Banquo and Macbeth did –

Mae

Macbeth?

Bloody Soldier

Redouble their blows on the foe like they meant to bathe themselves in blood –

Carlin

So they won?

Bloody Soldier
If you attend to the message –

Carlin
The message is a little hard on the ear.

Missy
Did they win?

Bloody Soldier
We won, aye.
We won. And Cawdor the traitor has been captured and
before the day is gone –

Carlin
Did you win?

Bloody Soldier
Me?

Mae
Aye, did you win?

Bloody Soldier
Of course I won, Scotland has my loyalty – so.

Carlin
Aye but did you really?

Bloody Soldier
I . . .

He looks at his arms and face.

The blood right down his side.

Mae puts up a chair for him.

I can't feel my feet.

Carlin
Ah.

Bloody Soldier
And my arms are tingling.

7

Carlin
Give him some tea, Missy.

Bloody Soldier
What happened to Cawdor?

Carlin
You tell me.

He retches.

He looks at all of them.

Bloody Soldier
Oh fuck –

Two of the weird sisters grab him.

He shouts in pain.

They move him, he shouts again.

I know who you are –

Missy
He knows who we are!

Carlin
Say nothing more –

Bloody Soldier
You shouldn't be here – you were told to leave the land.

Carlin
And go where?

They drop him.

He starts to crawl away.

Oh your legs move now –
You can scuttle like a beetle when you want to.
Put a foot on his back, Missy.

Missy puts a foot on his back.

Missy

Fair is foul and foul is fair. Crawl through the fog and filthy air –

Mae giggles.

Bloody Soldier

I have a message to deliver, I have to get to the king –

Carlin

Then message the king –

He tries to crawl away, can't.

But first – a drum a drum, Macbeth doth come.

Carlin crouches down, she holds his head.

He cries out in pain.

Say it –
Hail Macbeth, Thane of Glamis –

Bloody Soldier

Hail Macbeth, Thane of Glamis –

Missy

Hail Macbeth, Thane of Cawdor –

Bloody Soldier

Hail Macbeth, Thane of Cawdor –

Mae

Hail Macbeth, who will be king hereafter.

She drops him down, he falls.

Bloody Soldier

I won't, whatever hellish game you play.

Missy

We'll catch your wife, we'll boil your baby in the fire –

Bloody Soldier

So you are what they say –

He crawls away.

She grabs him again.

Carlin
Hail to thee.

Bloody Soldier
Hail to thee, Thane of Glamis.

Missy
Hail to thee.

Bloody Soldier
Hail to thee, Thane of Cawdor.

Mae
Hail to thee.

Bloody Soldier
Hail to thee, who will be king hereafter.

Macbeth and Banquo come on to the stage, fresh from battle.

Macbeth
Someone spoke – did you hear it?

Banquo
Aye, there's a man on the ground –

Bloody Soldier
I'm dead, I'm gone – do not give my words your ear –

The man crawls away –

Macbeth
Wait – you seemed to greet me as Cawdor –

Bloody Soldier
It wasn't me.

Macbeth
And then king.

Bloody Soldier
Three women stand behind you.
Anything that I spoke came from them –

Macbeth
How can that be?

Bloody Soldier
This is a cursed place, I don't know but –

Banquo
He's confused.

Bloody Soldier
The day is confused, undone. Look at the sky – both
things in one.

He crawls away.

Macbeth
Well . . .? Speak – he said his words came from you.

Macbeth
Glamis I am, he called me Cawdor I am certain –

Banquo
And king hereafter –

Missy
King.

Carlin
King.

Mae
King.

Carlin
Macbeth shall be king.

Macbeth
In the name of truth what are you?

Banquo

If you can look into the seeds of time and say which grain will grow speak then to me –

Carlin

Banquo, hail.

Missy

Hail Banquo.

Mae

Hail.

Carlin

Lesser than Macbeth, and greater.

Missy

Not so happy, yet much happier.

Banquo

What –

Mae

You shall get kings though you be none.

Banquo

Shall get kings?

They look at each other.

Macbeth

Stay a while, you imperfect speakers – tell us more –

They look around, the fog has returned.

Macbeth

I know I am Thane of Glamis but how of –?
The Thane of Cawdor lives, and to be king stands not within the prospect of belief, no more than Cawdor.
Speak –

The women have gone.

Banquo

Whither are they vanished?

Macbeth

Into the air, and what seemed corporal, melted as breath into the wind.

They look around again.

Banquo

Have we eaten on the insane root that takes the reason prisoner?

Macbeth

I cannot work it out. Your children shall be kings.

Banquo

You shall be king.

Macbeth

And Thane of Cawdor too –

Banquo

To the self-same tune and words.

Macbeth

We came for water, let's get it then leave this place.

Ross comes on.

Ross

Macbeth, the king hath happily received the news of thy success.

Macbeth

Ah!

Ross

And when he reads thy personal venture in the rebels' fight, his wonders and praises do contend what should be thine or his.

Macbeth

The service and loyalty I owe, in doing it, pays itself.

Ross

And for an earnest of a greater honour, he bade me, from him call thee Thane of Cawdor in which addition –

Macbeth

Whoa –

Ross

Hail most worthy thane, for it is thine –

Banquo

Can the devil speak true?

Macbeth

The Thane of Cawdor lives. Why do you dress me in borrowed robes?

Ross

Who was the thane lives yet, but under heavy judgement and treason is capital. So. Come to the king, he wishes to greet and thank you himself –

Macbeth

I will.

Ross slaps Macbeth's back and leaves.

Macbeth and Banquo look at each other.

Banquo

Cawdor!

Macbeth

And your children kings – those that gave the Thane of Cawdor to me promised no less to them?

Banquo

It's strange, I admit, but –

Macbeth

Strange? I'm the Thane of fucking Cawdor. This supernatural soliciting cannot be ill, can it? Cannot be good, but if ill, why hath it given me an earnest of success commencing with a truth?

Banquo
I do not know.

Macbeth
But if good, why does it make my seated heart knock at my ribs?

Beat.

Let us toward the king. Think upon what has chanced, and at more time, the interim having weighted it, let us speak of our free hearts each to other.

Banquo
Very gladly.

Macbeth
Till then, enough.

Banquo
Aye, enough.

They walk off – Banquo ahead.

Macbeth turns back to look at what has just happened.

Carlin seems to speak the thoughts in his mind.

Carlin
Stars, hide your fires, let not light see my black and deep desires.
The eye winks at the hand; yet let that be which the eye fears, when it is done to see.

Macbeth backs away, frightened by what he heard out loud.

The other two women laugh.

TWO

Lady Macbeth turns on a light above her head.

She reads aloud a letter.

Lady Macbeth
'They met me in the day of success, and I have learned by the perfectest report, they have more in them than mortal knowledge. When I burned in desire to question them further, they made themselves air; into which they vanished.'

She puts the letter down.

My love. Glamis you are, and Cawdor, and shalt be what thou art promised. Yet do I fear thy nature, it is too full o'th' milk of human kindness to catch the nearest way. Thou wouldst be great, art not without ambition, but without that illness should attend it.

She opens the letter again – looks at it.

Come you spirits that tend on mortal thoughts, unsex me here and fill me from the crown to the toe, top-full of direst cruelty.
Then my lord.
Hie thee hither that I may pour *my* spirit in thine ear –

Macbeth enters and stands in the doorway.

Macbeth
Kiss me.

Lady Macbeth
Great Glamis, worthy Cawdor, greater than both by the all-hail hereafter –

They kiss.

Macbeth
You read the letter?

Lady Macbeth
I feel now the future in the instant.

Macbeth
Dearest love.

And kiss again.

And laugh.

Duncan comes here tonight.

Lady Macbeth
So soon?

Beat.

And when goes hence?

Macbeth
Tomorrow as he purposes.

Beat.

Lady Macbeth
O never sun shall that morrow see.

Beat.

They look at each other

Your face, my thane, is as a book where anyone may read
strange matters; to beguile the time, look like the time,
bear welcome in your eye, your hand, your tongue; look
like the innocent flower but be the serpent under it.

They kiss again.

Macbeth
We will speak further.

Lady Macbeth
Only look up clear. To alter favour ever is to fear.

This kiss is sexier. They both lean in.

There's excitement. Can they mean it?

Wait –

Macbeth
What?

Lady Macbeth
There.
On your sleeve.

She takes off an insect.

A ladybird.
Ha!
A sign of luck!

Macbeth
A ladybird in Scotland?

Lady Macbeth
Well, does it not feel like summer today?

Macbeth
Too early in the year.
Another strange soliciting –

He takes the ladybird and puts it on the side.

Did you move all your papers, by the way – this whole
house was full of your writings –

Lady Macbeth
I'll do it now –

Macbeth
Because if the king happens upon any of it –

Lady Macbeth
We are his most loyal supporters, we always have been.

The raven cries.

I'll tell the kitchen steward to roast a pheasant. Or perhaps,
no wait, a goose might be better for Duncan – see if we
have one hanging or –

He comes back, kisses her.

Macbeth
I love you.

Lady Macbeth
And I, you.

THREE

The Carlin from the first scene is putting the ladybird back into a box.

She then takes off her outdoor clothes.

Carlin
We were at the end of days but who were we to tell them? Inside, the fire was on but without heat. And up at the top the servant, hands cold, always cold and an injury that never healed.

She looks at her hands.

And a rattle, always a rattle in this old place that she could never work out, like something didn't fit, and just then a chimney was blown down.
And strange lamentings heard in the air – screams of death that she had neither interpretation not appetite to digest –

She puts on a servant's dress. Tries to warm her hands.

And the obscure bird clamoured outside the window the livelong night.

She holds her hands again. The pain.

And yet downstairs a party. Duncan couldn't hear the screams of the birds over the sound of his own delight –

She takes some tea.

A slight knocking.

Carlin has become the servant.

Servant
Aye it made no sense.

She stops the table from being wobbly.

She sits back down.

The birds screaming out death while they were dancing –

FOUR

Table laid for a party. Balloons and streamers.

Duncan
This castle has a pleasant seat . . . the air nimbly and
sweetly recommends itself to my gentle senses.

Lady Macduff
Ah, the birds agree, and hence – they take the best
lodgings as their own.

Duncan
The birds –?

Lady Macduff
Yes – the guest of summer, the martlet – see – by his loved
masonry.

Duncan looks around –

No part of wall, buttress, but this bird has made its
pendent bed –

Duncan
Ah.

Lady Macduff
And there – the choughs, and behind them the corncrakes.

Duncan
You are well studied in the way of birds.

Lady Macduff
We are all studied in their way, your grace. They rule us in this keep.
But sir, take care – the other side of their living is not so welcome –

She points at the bird shit underfoot.

He laughs.

And in the night too, they sing the loudest, they'll keep you up with tales of their day –

Duncan
I sleep too well to listen to much.

Lady Macduff
No one misses their lullaby here –

She makes the sound of a bird.

Duncan is amused.

Lady Macduff, at your humble service.

Duncan
Macduff? Ah. Your husband is dear to me –

Lady Macduff
As I will be then. Doubly so. Only I have been sent to delay your royal entrance by my sister just so you don't see the full brouhaha on the other side of the door.

She mimes – the king is coming – panic!

Duncan laughs again.

Duncan
You're enchanting, you know that? Macduff is a lucky man.

Lady Macduff
Tell that to Macduff.

Duncan
Oh I will when I see him –

Lady Macduff

Exactly – when you see him!

Malcolm

Father –

Duncan

Ah, the rest of my company arriving now – Excuse me.

Malcolm, Ross and Lennox arrive, a bit out of breath from the climb up.

Ross

My lord –

Duncan turns away from Lady Macduff and towards Ross.

Duncan

Is execution done on Cawdor? Or not those in commission yet returned?

Ross

I have spoke with one who saw him die, who did report that very frankly he confessed his treasons, implored your highness' pardon –

Duncan

Aha?

Lennox

And set forth a deep repentance.

Duncan

But he is dead?

Ross

Aye he died, sir.

Duncan

Son, come here. Sort yourself out.

Enter Lady Macbeth.

Lady Macbeth
Forgive me, I had not heard that you had yet arrived.

Lady Macduff
I entertained him as you said –

Duncan
No matter.

Lady Macbeth
Your speed surprised us – welcome at last –

She bows.

All our service, done and then done double, were poor and single business to contend against those honours deep and broad wherewith your majesty loads our house.

Duncan
You know my son.

Lady Macbeth
Malcolm, of course – come in, come in –

They embrace.

Duncan
Where's the Thane of Cawdor himself?! We coursed him at the heels, but he rides well –

Lady Macbeth
He checks the wine I think –

Lady Macduff
What, the cellars not ready for royal tasting?

Lady Macbeth
Here they come.

Macbeth and Banquo arrive, Macbeth carrying wine –

Duncan
Macbeth, you old devil –

Macbeth
Your grace.

Duncan
So fast on a horse, come here. And Banquo no less
deserving –

Duncan embraces them both.

Well, put your arms around me, we're family now.

The embrace takes them by surprise.

It's fulsome and firm.

Lady Macduff
Banquo.

Banquo
Lady Duff.

Duncan
Assembled then. My son, family, thanes. Let's throw away
formality –

He holds up his glass as if to start a toast.

Yes I'm your king, but today –

A bird sounds loudly.

What's that?

They look around.

Macbeth
A bird has come inside.

Malcolm
I don't like birds –

Lady Macbeth
No matter – I'll deal with it –

Lennox
It makes a racket –

Ross
Perhaps Cawdor's spirit coming to piss on the party −!

Malcolm
Cawdor −?

Banquo
As a sparrow?

Lady Macduff
It's a starling.

Macbeth
Or a chough.

Ross
Where is it?

Lady Macbeth
In the rafter − fear not − they do this sometimes.

Lady Macduff
I was telling our royal friend about the birds −

Lady Macbeth
Yes it seems we are oddly favoured − please as you were −

Malcolm
Get it out.

Duncan
Alright, son −

Lady Macbeth goes to reach for it −

Macbeth
It will be gone in a moment −

Malcolm
Unless it pecks our eyes out.

Lennox
A little thing like that −?

Lady Macduff
See it as nature come to join our feast −

Malcolm
I don't care for nature –

The bird makes more noise – Lady Macbeth has taken a chair.

Lady Macbeth
There, it's gone –

Malcolm
Not yet –

Lady Macbeth
Well, so I thought –

Malcolm
It flew by this way –

Banquo
Yes and out the window –

Ross
If it was Cawdor – it would not have been so biddable –!

Beat.

Malcolm
Has it gone, Father?

Duncan
Aye it's gone.
But be a man and don't cower so – if it was Cawdor, the worst he can do to you now is shite and flap –

Lady Macbeth
The old Cawdor – the new sits amongst us!

Duncan
Indeed.

Macbeth
Whoever it was, it's now to the wild returned.

Lady Macbeth
And the window is now shut, so –

They listen – nothing.

Lady Macbeth comes back to the table.

Duncan
A new toast –

Lady Macduff throws a streamer.

To the Macbeths – see, son, the heroes of the hour. Not
only does *he* save our crown upon the battlefield but *she*
saves our good cheer from a passing chough.
Honoured hosts – to you – lord and lady – the new
Cawdors.

They all raise a glass.

And say together:

All
The new Cawdors!

FIVE

*The kitchen. Macbeth is opening some wine; sounds of the
party in the background.*

Macbeth
If it were done when 'tis done, then 'twere well it were
done quickly.
If th'assassination could trammel up all consequence and
catch with his surcease, success: that but this blow might
be the be-all and end-all here – and here instead on this
bank and shoal of time, we jump the life to come –

*Lady Macbeth has appeared; she takes the bottle of wine
from him and opens it.*

Lady Macbeth
He has almost supped. Why do you not return – ?

Macbeth
Has he asked for me?

Lady Macbeth
Know you not, he has?

Macbeth
We should proceed no further in this business: he has honoured me of late, and I have bought golden opinions, which would be worn now in their newest gloss, not cast aside so soon.

Lady Macbeth
What? Was the hope drunk wherein you dressed yourself? Has it slept since? And wakes it now to look so green and pale at what it did so freely?

Macbeth
We like him not, but to do this –

Lady Macbeth
Are you not the sole reason he breathes this evening? What might have happened today if you and Banquo had not met success? Would we wake up and find we are Norwegian?

Macbeth
He does what he does –

Lady Macbeth
What is it that halts you my love? Fear? Are you afraid to be the same in what you do and what you want and what you might become? Letting 'I dare not' wait upon 'I would' like the poor cat in the adage?

Macbeth
Please, stop –

Lady Macbeth
Why when you dare not?

Macbeth
I dare.

I dare do all that may become a man. Who dares do more, is none.

Lady Macbeth
What beast was't then that made you break this enterprise to me? When you durst do it, then you were a man; and to be more than what you were, you would be so much more the man. Nor time nor place did then adhere, and yet you would make both: they have made themselves, and that their fitness now does unmake you –

Macbeth
He dines in our chamber, I am his host.

Lady Macbeth
So? I have given suck, have I not? And I know how tender it is to love the babe that milks me: I would, while it was smiling in my face, have plucked the nipple from its boneless gums and dashed the brains out, had I so sworn as you have done to this.

Macbeth
I haven't sworn.

Lady Macbeth
You've said you might.

Macbeth
So by saying I might, I have promised?

Beat.

Lady Macbeth
Look at me.

She takes his face into her hands.

Look at me.

He looks at her.

Pause.

They breathe into each other.

The king is here for a single night.
We can do this.

Macbeth
And if we should fail?

Lady Macbeth
We fail.
But screw your courage to the sticking place and we'll
not fail.

Banquo comes to the door.

Banquo
Are you coming back in?

Lady Macbeth
Banquo! We will just be a moment –

She passes him the wine bottle.

Take in this wine – make sure everyone's glass is full.

Banquo goes back in.

Macbeth
Bring forth men-children only, for your undaunted mettle
should make only males.

He kisses her. Then he looks at his hands.

I am settled. And bend up each corporal agent to this
terrible feat.

She kisses his hands.

Lady Macbeth
Away and mock the time with fairest show.
Yes?

Outside noise comes from the party – it sounds like music.

False face.

Macbeth
    Ha.
    False face must hide what the false heart doth know.

She kisses him and leaves.

The sound of the party is getting louder, everyone is enjoying themselves, and drunk.

They go and join in the celebration.

SIX

The servant catches Lady Macbeth on her way back to the table.

Servant
    Some women stand at the gate, madam.

Lady Macbeth
    Well, who let them in?

Servant
    They say they were told to come and you'd give them a welcome.

Lady Macbeth
    What sort of welcome?

Servant
    They want to speak to you –

Lady Macbeth
    I don't have time for this – surely you could have determined that without calling for my attention?

Servant
    They cursed me as I told them not to enter – they said things that filled my head –

Lady Macbeth
Heed not their curses, curses only work on the believer.

Servant
What shall I say then?

Beat.

Lady Macbeth
Say the lady cannot speak with them tonight. That is what you say.
And then you lock the gate.

Lady Macbeth takes the tray of glasses and walks away.

She drops the glasses.

Blast –

Lady Macduff has wandered out –

Lady Macduff
Everything okay?

Lady Macbeth
Yes. Just butter fingers – nothing.

Lady Macduff comes over, helps her pick the glasses up.

Lady Macduff
Careful you don't cut yourself.

They both bend down to clear up the glass.

Lady Macbeth
Get to bed early – don't stay up late, will you?

Lady Macduff
I'll stay up for as long as anyone does.

Lady Macbeth
Of course, but after that – get some sleep.

Lady Macduff
I always do.

Lady Macbeth
I'm thinking of my young nephew, that's all. A new baby in the house –

She puts her hand on the bump.

Lady Macduff
Or niece.

Lady Macbeth
Indeed. Either!

Lady Macduff puts her hand over Lady Macbeth's.

A noise.

It makes them both start.

They laugh.

The bloody choughs.

Lady Macduff
Be merry tonight, coz, the party goes well –

Lady Macbeth
I know it.

Around the table, someone has started to sing.

Lady Macduff
Come on, let's go and have a dance –

The singing around the table has become rowdy. Someone moves the table and gets out a tin whistle. Someone else starts to dance. Lady Macduff hitches her skirt up and joins in.

SEVEN

Later.

The party is over. Banquo sits.

Macbeth comes in to clear the table.

Macbeth
Not yet at rest? The king's abed –

Banquo
The king – ffft – unusual pleasure! Sent forth great largess
to your household. The diamond he greets your wife with –

Macbeth
I think it was the wine and not the wife he meant to honour!

Macbeth
I'll drink to that!

Banquo
Drink what? Our sovereign drank the lot –

They laugh together.

Macbeth starts to clear away some of the debris.

I can't stop thinking of those weird sisters –

Macbeth
Tchh – think not of them.

Banquo
Really? To you they have showed some truth.

Macbeth
I suppose, aye.

Beat.

Banquo
I've hardly thought about much else, in all honesty.

Macbeth
Where's your boy?

Banquo

Fleance? Sleeping I hope.

Macbeth

If I do become king – whenever that day is –

Banquo

Sounds like politicking of a king already.

Macbeth

If you shall cleave to my consent when 'tis the time –

Banquo

My support for you is constant, you know that, whatever role or promotion finds you.

Macbeth

Thank you.

Banquo

As long as I keep my bosom franchised and allegiance clear.

Beat.

Macbeth

Of course.

Banquo

Then I shall be counselled, aye.

Beat. Macbeth isn't sure what his friend is saying.

Macbeth

Thy friendship is dearest of all to me.

Banquo

And to me, dear one.

Macbeth

Goodnight.

Banquo

Thanks sir, the like to you.

Macbeth watches his friend go.

The servant comes in and starts clearing the table.

Macbeth
> Go bid thy mistress, when my drink is ready she strike upon
> the bell. And then get yourself to bed. It's been a long night –

Servant
> Thank you, sir.

Macbeth nods and watches as the servant leaves.

He is left with all the debris.

He sits down.

He takes a knife from on the table.

Plays with it. Twirls with it in his hand.

The bird is back in the room.

Macbeth
> I'm sure my lady had put you out the window.
> What? I pick up a knife and you appear.

He tries to reach it, but the bird isn't there –

> Cawdor is that you? Come to meet your treachery with
> mine – and cheer me on now as traitor? I see you yet in
> form but cannot touch you –

He tries and can't.

> It is the bloody business then which informs thus to mine
> eyes. You are but a false creation – now o'er the one half-
> world nature seems dead, and wicked dreams abuse the
> curtained sleep; witchcraft celebrates, and withered
> murder thus with his stealthy pace towards his design
> moves like a ghost.
> Go, bird of hell, Cawdor's spirit, I see you not –

He swipes at the bird, the dagger falls to the floor.

The sound of it clattering on the floor seems to be too loud.

He puts his hands over his ears. The bell joins in.

I go and it is done, the bell invites me.
Hear it not, Duncan, for it is a knell that summons thee to
heaven or to hell.

EIGHT

Lady Macbeth comes into the kitchen.

She reaches for a drink.

Lady Macbeth
That which has made them drunk, has made me bold;
what has quenched them, has given me fire.

There is a noise. She jumps.

Hark! Peace.

*She calms herself down, realises that she is on high alert,
she's being daft.*

It was the owl that shrieked.
He is about it. The doors are open and the grooms do
mock their charge with snores. Possets so drugged that
death and life do contend about them.
I laid their daggers ready; he could not miss them. My
husband?

Macbeth comes in.

Macbeth
Didst thou hear a noise?

Lady Macbeth
I heard the owl scream and the crickets cry.
Did you not speak?

Macbeth
When?

37

Lady Macbeth
Now.

Macbeth
As I descended –

Lady Macbeth
Aye.
Have you done the deed?

Macbeth
Aye. Who lies in the second bedroom?

Lady Macbeth
Malcolm and Ross.

Macbeth
This is a sorry sight.

Lady Macbeth
A foolish thought to say a sorry sight.

Macbeth
There's one that did laugh in his sleep, and one cried
'Murder'.

Lady Macbeth
These deeds must not be thought after these ways; so it
will make us mad.

Macbeth
Methought I heard a voice cry 'Sleep no more.
Macbeth does murder sleep.'

Lady Macbeth
Tchh.

Macbeth
The innocent sleep, sleep that knits up the ravelled sleave
of care, the death of each day's life, balm of hurt minds.

Lady Macbeth
What do you mean?

Macbeth

Still it cried 'Sleep no more' to all the house; 'Glamis hath
murdered sleep, and therefore Cawdor shall sleep no more.'

Lady Macbeth

Why, worthy thane, do you unbend your noble strength to
think so brainsickly of things? Go and get some water and
wash this filthy witness from your hand.

He starts to go.

Wait – why did you bring these daggers from the place?
They must lie there.

Macbeth

What?

Lady Macbeth

Good grief, go carry them and smear the sleepy grooms
with blood.

Macbeth

I'll go no more.

Lady Macbeth

Go now –

Macbeth

I'm afraid to think what I have done. Look on it again,
no – I dare not.

Lady Macbeth

Infirm of purpose, give me the daggers then. The sleeping
and the dead are but as pictures; 'tis the eye of childhood
that fears a painted devil. If he do bleed, I'll gild the faces
of the grooms with it for it must seem their guilt.

Macbeth

Whence is that knocking?

Lady Macbeth

I can't hear it.

Macbeth

There.

Lady Macbeth

Nothing.

She leaves.

He listens again.

There is a knocking.

The knocking seems too loud.

Macbeth

How is it with me, when every noise appals me? What hands are here? Ha: they pluck out mine eyes. Will all great Neptune's ocean wash this blood clean from my hand? No – this my hand will rather the multitudinous seas incarnadine, making the green run red.

Lady Macbeth comes back in.

Lady Macbeth

My hands are of your colour, look, but I shame to wear a heart so white. Retire we to our chamber – a little water clears us of this deed.

Macbeth

More knocking –

Lady Macbeth

Get on your nightgown, lest occasion call us and show us to be watchers. Be not lost so poorly in your thoughts.

Macbeth

To know my deed, it were best not know myself. Wake Duncan with your knocking. I would you could.

NINE

Banquo and Lady Macduff are flirting, kissing in the corridors.

Knocking in the background is loud.

Lady Macduff
Shush, no one must see us –

Banquo
Here's a knocking indeed –

Lady Macduff
Too early for a caller –
If a man were porter of Hell Gate, he would grow old
turning the key.

Giggly.

More knocks.

Banquo
Knock knock knock!

Lady Macduff
You should devil porter it.

Banquo
Who is there in the name of Belzebub?

Lady Macduff
Whoever you are, begone and get back to the grave.

They laugh, more kissing.

More knocking.

Banquo
Maybe we should answer it?

Lady Macduff
Let his household deal with callers –

Banquo
But as his loyal allies –

Lady Macduff
Do you always do what he bids you?

Banquo
He didn't bid me do this, did he?

They go back into a clinch.

More knocking.

Lady Macduff
Stop the endless knocking. Where the hell is the porter?

Banquo
Drunk!

Lady Macduff
Like the rest of us –

They laugh and fall into each other.

Lady Macduff's necklace breaks – the beads roll all over the floor.

Oh God, these were a wedding gift – if I lose them –

She starts to pick them up.

Banquo opens the door.

Macduff
About bloody time, you had me standing out there for hours.

He sees Lady Macduff.

My lady.

Lady Macduff
My lord.
We had expected you yesterday.

Macduff
Glad to see you have been kept entertained.
Banquo.

Banquo
Macduff.
The king is within.

Macduff
Of course he is and that asked me to come and get him up
betimes.

He looks at Lady Macduff and Banquo.

Isn't quite sure what to make of it.

Beat.

This place stinks of booze, by the way.
You stink of booze.
And something else –

He smells him.

Banquo
Victory?

Macduff
Vomit I think.
I had meant to arrive in time for the feast, of course I did,
but –

Lady Macduff
Is the king leaving today then?

Macduff
He is, he asked me to make sure he could get away early,
before the lark –

Lady Macduff
So you won't stay?
You'll go with him?

Macduff
I will yes.

Macduff comes and gives her a kiss.

We'll be together soon, yes?

Lady Macduff
I can hardly wait.

Macduff
How's the child?

Lady Macduff
Oh our babe you mean, our potential son and heir?
Will you make his birth?

Macduff
If I am not needed elsewhere –

Lady Macduff
Well, I will tell our child not to appear at a moment that
unduly inconveniences his father.

Beat.

Macduff leaves.

Banquo raises an eyebrow –

Don't!

Macbeth comes down –

Macbeth
What's all the knocking –?

Lady Macduff
My Lord Macduff is returned, wants the king up and
early –

Macbeth
What are you two doing up?

Lady Macduff
The night was full of strange noises, did you hear –

Banquo
I couldn't sleep.

Macbeth
Strange, I slept well –

Macbeth gets a glass of milk.

Macduff re-enters.

Macduff
Jesus –

Banquo
What's the matter?

Macduff
I –
Get everyone up –

Macbeth
You're making no sense.

Macduff
There is no sense – go through to his chamber and see for yourselves.

Macbeth leaves.

Get them awake, would you – Ross. Lennox. Malcolm, anyone who is here – Up, up, death is amongst us.

Banquo
Death?

Macduff
Aye, death. Ring the bell.

Lady Macduff goes to strike the bell.

Banquo
Please – tell me.

Macduff
See for yourself.

Banquo
Duncan?

Macduff
Aye, Duncan. Slaughtered.

Lady Macbeth comes in, in her nightgown.

Lady Macbeth
What is it that so much noise calls to wake the sleepers of the house?

Macduff
Oh, gentle lady.

Lady Macbeth
Speak, speak –

Lady Macduff
Our royal master is murdered.

Lennox
What?

Lady Macbeth
In our house?

Lady Macduff
Too cruel anywhere. Dear Duff, is this right?

Macduff
Aye.

Macbeth
Had I but died an hour before, I would say I had lived in a blessed time, but now all that is as –

Lady Macbeth
It's true then?

Macbeth
His grace is dead, yes.

Ross
That can't be – when?

Macbeth
Well how can we know – he's dead now.

Macduff
Go – see for yourself.

Malcolm
What's amiss?

Lennox
You are, and do not know it.

Macbeth
The fountain of your blood is stopped; the very source of it stopped.

Malcolm
What?

Banquo
Your royal father's murdered.

Lady Macduff
Don't tell the child.

Banquo
He has to know.

Malcolm
By whom?

Macduff
Those of his chamber, it seems. Their hands and faces were all covered with his blood; so were their daggers, which unwiped we found upon their pillows.

Malcolm
But – my father.

Banquo
We'll drag them here and put some questions to them –

Macbeth
Oh yet I do repent of my fury, that I did kill them –

Macduff
What?

Banquo
Why?

Macbeth

Because who can be wise, amazed, temperate and furious, loyal and neutral, in a moment? You? Ffftt! Here lay Duncan, his silver skin laced with his golden blood; there, the murderers –

Lady Macbeth

Help me, oh I feel faint.

Banquo

Look to the lady –

Lady Macbeth faints.

Banquo

She needs to be aided back to bed.

Lady Macduff

I'll take her.

Lady Macduff helps Lady Macbeth off.

Banquo

And when we have caught our breath and the naked frailties of our distress are once again hidden – let us meet and question what has happened here. Fears and doubts shake us all. But in the great hand of God I stand, and will find and fight the pretence of treasonous malice.

Macduff

And so do I.

Macbeth

And I.

Banquo

Let's quickly dress ourselves as befits the day and meet together in the hall.

All

Aye.

TEN

Macbeth grabs Banquo and has a word with him.

Macbeth
Why lead the men so?

Banquo
Lead the men where?

Macbeth
This is my house, and yet you took the charge.
If a council is to be had then let me cry it.

Banquo
I am loyal, you know I am.

Beat.

Macbeth
My apologies. I know you are.

Banquo
Friend?

Macbeth
Aye.

Banquo
Why *did* you kill them, though, the men of his chamber?

Macbeth
I told you –

Banquo
'Emotion'?

Macbeth
Yes. They slew the king. Of course emotion.

Beat.

And they slew him here in my house. My castle where he
was our guest. What host would I be if my anger had not
moved me so –?

Banquo looks at him.

Banquo
Of course.
'Tis a pity though, eh? They live not to be questioned.

Macbeth
Aye yes, 'tis a pity.

Macbeth looks at Banquo. Puts a hand on his chest.

Then leaves.

Banquo calls over Malcolm.

Banquo
What will you do?
Let's not consort with them –

Malcolm
I don't know – my father.

Banquo
As his heir –

Malcolm
I cannot stay – I understand but –

Banquo
This murderous shaft that's shot hath not yet lighted, and
safest way is to avoid the aim. Not only that, but you as
the one who has the most to gain.

Malcolm
Where to go though?

Banquo
England. Quick to horse and don't be dainty of leave-
taking but shift away.

Banquo takes out some money and gives it to him.

Malcolm takes it.

There's daggers in men's smiles. Now go.

Malcolm leaves.

Macduff comes in.

Macduff
Where did you send the boy – ?

Banquo
Not a boy, a man surely?

Macduff
Duncan's appointed heir, aye, where did you send him?

Beat.

Oh come on, you don't trust me? Where?

Lady Macbeth brings in an armful of flowers.

She puts them in a vase.

Banquo watches her.

And Macduff.

She notices them looking at her.

Lady Macbeth
Macduff. Banquo.

They smile back.

She leaves.

Banquo
England.

Macduff leaves. Banquo is left alone for a second.

He wonders if that was the right thing to do.

ELEVEN

The three servants appear.

They look at each other.

They clear away the debris.

Servant

'Tis a funny thing – the crap they throw. The revolting
shite they leave behind. The place in the morning. The way
they leave at night, imagining that some unnatural spirit
will enter and pick it up in the dark, perhaps so that
miraculously it is all pressed and new formed by dawn,
not sprites but people, aye but they don't see the bottles
half-empty, vomit on occasion, meat half-chewed and spat
into the corner – this one likes not to eat the gristle, and
this one does not like the meat too rare – if they could,
they would have us chew it for them first, then spit it back
so that they might more easily digest. And we, what, hover
through the fog and filthy air? See what's rotting in the
lair, oh sweltered venom sleeping got, boil thou first i'th'
charmed pot. Poisoned entrails, days and night, eye of
newt and dog of flight.

Lady Macbeth comes in, with her dress undone at the back.

Lady Macbeth

Here –
Can you help me into this?

The woman helps her. Does up the buttons.

Thank you.

The woman carries on scrubbing.

Lady Macbeth puts on her shoes.

She looks at the woman.

The woman looks at her.

If there is anything else I'll call you.

Servant
Very good.

The servant picks up her bucket and goes away.

Macbeth comes in, trying to do up his cufflinks.

Lady Macbeth goes over to Macbeth and helps him.

He lets her.

Beat.

He takes out his tie and starts to put it on.

Macbeth
To be thus is nothing, but to be safely thus.

Lady Macbeth
We are safely thus.

Macbeth
Are we?

She helps him do up his tie.

Lady Macbeth
Aye we are.

Macbeth
Banquo, where is he?
I told him, we desired his good advice today –

Lady Macbeth
Tonight we hold a solemn supper, let's request his presence then.

Beat.

Macbeth sits down on the edge of the bed.

Macbeth
Our fears in Banquo stick deep. 'Tis much he dares do, and has a dauntless manner – a royalty of nature that is made to be feared –

Lady Macbeth

Banquo?

Macbeth

He chid the sisters when first they put the name of king on me, and made them speak to him. Then, prophet-like, they hailed him father to a line of kings.

Lady Macbeth

What?

Macbeth

Upon my head they placed a fruitless crown, no son of mine succeeding, but for Banquo a full royal lineage. If this is so, then for Banquo's children have I defiled my mind?

Lady Macbeth

Banquo's children?

Macbeth

Yes, for them, and not ours, the gracious Duncan I have murdered.

Lady Macbeth

Whence came this intelligence?

Macbeth

Aye, the women said it was for them I put poison in the vessel of my peace, only for them; and my immortal soul sold to Satan to make them kings, the seeds of Banquo kings.

Lady Macbeth

And not our own?

Macbeth

No, not our own.

Lady Macbeth

So for Fleance then?

Macbeth

Aye for Fleance, I suppose, yes for Fleance.

Lady Macbeth
His son?

Banquo comes in.

Banquo
I heard 'tis most likely the sovereignty will fall upon you,
Macbeth.

Macbeth
I am already named, yes.

Banquo
Congratulations. And you go this day to Scone to be
invested?

Macbeth
Yes, we prepare now for a service of thanksgiving in the
castle, then –

Banquo
All so soon?

Lady Macbeth
Not soon enough when the country lies without a king –

Banquo
Where is Duncan's body?

Lady Macbeth
Where do you think, Banquo?

Macbeth
Carried to Colmekill and soon buried.

Banquo
The speed of the arrangements leaves me somewhat
surprised –

Macbeth
Efficiency, the country cannot be without a head for long.

Lady Macbeth
And on which note, tonight we hold a formal supper, sir,
a feast – and we request your presence.

Banquo
Me?

Lady Macbeth
Our chief guest.

Macbeth
How could I have a banquet without you there?

Banquo
Let your highness command upon me, then – you know
my duty is to you forever knit.

Macbeth
Thank you.
Ride you this afternoon?

Banquo
Aye, my good sir.

Macbeth
We should have else desired your presence at the service.

Lady Macbeth
Is it far you ride?

Banquo
As far as will fill up the time 'twixt this and supper.

Macbeth
Fail not our feast.

Banquo
I will not.

He leaves.

Macbeth looks at Lady Macbeth.

Macbeth
We have scorched the snake, not killed it: she'll close and
join one end to the other, whilst our weak malice remains
in danger of her former tooth.

They look at each other.

Lady Macbeth
Why was it that you did not tell me?

Macbeth
I told you all I needed to tell you.

Lady Macbeth
But no, sir, it was not so, for our children –

Macbeth
We have no children.

Lady Macbeth
Living.
We have no children living.
But with time and God's blessing –

Macbeth
Don't bother my head now –

Lady Macbeth
Bother your head? If not for our children then for what –

Macbeth
We have no children, do we?
We have no children, so if Fleance gets it –

Lady Macbeth
But we will.

They look at each other.

We will.

Hymn books are handed out – the Macbeths are at the service in the chapel. They sing a couple of lines of a sombre hymn – the whole company joins in.

Macbeth and Lady Macbeth snatch a few more seconds to talk.

Macbeth
Full of scorpions is my mind, dear wife –

Lady Macbeth
Then talk to me?

Macbeth
And what, say things you do not want to hear?

Lady Macbeth
This country pleads for you, Scotland cries out for a
steadying hand – so let them have it. Good counsel we will
take, advice, we will be wise, temperate, fair and true –

Macbeth
Let your remembrance apply to Banquo.

Lady Macbeth
Banquo again?
You must leave this, Banquo is not our problem but
Fleance –

*The organ music starts up again – more ceremonial religious
music.*

They have to wait before they can speak again.

Macbeth
There's comfort yet, they are assailable.

Lady Macbeth
What, both? Whence comes this thought?

They sit down and kneel.

Macbeth
Ere the bat hath flown his cloistered flight, there shall be
done a deed of dreadful note.

Lady Macbeth
What's to be done?

He makes the sign of the cross.

She follows suit.

Macbeth

Be innocent of the knowledge, dearest chuck, till thou
applaud the deed.

They receive the sacrament.

TWELVE

*Lady Macduff is getting herself into a dress. She talks to her
bump.*

Lady Macduff

Steady, little bird, or I'll do it tighter.
Or, if you want, kick now but then later, hear this.
However much we hate the day – we must be ready; it is
the occasion, not the dress that calls for us – oh stop!

She tries to do the dress tighter.

We're happy for my sister and her husband, aren't we? So
why is your kicking so different in its mood from this
morning?
And see – now even my necklace breaks and double
breaks –
Montrose will be there, our friends Kincardine, Birse, Cowie.
We will take our place amongst the thanes even if
Macduff will not join us – Arbuthnott knew my father,
your grandfather; Fettercairn, Menmuir.

Lady Macbeth comes in.

Lady Macbeth

Oh, I thought you would be ready by now.

Lady Macduff

Nearly.

Lady Macbeth

Isobel – the coronation feast is soon –

Lady Macduff
I know. It's the child that's slows me.

Lady Macbeth
He didn't like his uncle being made king –?

Lady Macduff
He did but perhaps the speed with which we turned from
our rueing to rejoicing left us a little unsteady, that's all –

Lady Macbeth
Unsteady? Isn't this turn the most steadying of all? After
so long, our politics and way of justice is coming – no
more wars and years of turmoil –

Lady Macduff
Just so quick.

Lady Macbeth
When is Macduff arriving?

Lady Macduff
I don't know – he hasn't sent word.

Lady Macbeth
He *is* coming?

Lady Macduff
How can I tell?
He hardly speaks to me.

Lady Macbeth
You will learn to love him, and he you. Of course you will.
When the child is born –

Lady Macduff
He says he won't accept the child unless it has his exact
eyes and face.

Beat.

Lady Macbeth
Why would he say that?

Lady Macduff shrugs.

Lady Macduff
Because he's bloody minded?

Lady Macbeth
The child is his?

Lady Macduff
Of course it is.

Lady Macbeth
Isobel, we both need a sister today, yes. Me for you and
you for me. We'll sit and talk through all of this,
I promise, but now I have to walk beside my husband and
stand like a queen.

Lady Macduff
Of course.

Lady Macbeth
In less than an hour. Later then, all of this?

Lady Macduff
Yes.

Lady Macbeth kisses her.

Lady Macbeth
I love you. I need you. Be calm.

Lady Macbeth goes to touch the bump.

And you, stop making your mother so sick. Come
celebrate your family!

Lady Macbeth leaves –

The servant catches her on the way out.

Servant
Those three women have been knocking at the gate again.

Lady Macbeth
Again?

Servant

They say now you are queen they need to speak.

Lady Macbeth

Did you not order them off the land last time?

Servant

I did.

Lady Macbeth

So why are they still there? Tell them we will set about them with dogs and fire if they don't go. Or worse. Acid and chemicals. Say whatever you need to say, but get them off our land.

Lady Macbeth leaves.

Lady Macduff looks at the servant.

Lady Macduff

Who are they?

The servant shrugs.

Servant

Just three women who sit and wait at the gate.

Lady Macduff

What do they want?

The servant shrugs.

Servant

I don't know. They're cold, hungry. They say they just want to speak to her.

Lady Macduff

Oh.
And did she not invite them in?

THIRTEEN

Music starts.

The stage is prepared for a celebration.

Chairs are put out, flowers. The servants chant off the names of those who will be attending.

Servant
Montrose? Coming.
Kincardine. Yes.
Birse, Cowie, Arbuthnott, Fettercairn, all in attendance.
Kinnaber on his way.
Menmuir, Clova, Kinalty, Tannadice, here.
Old Montrose – limping, needs a chair.
Menteith has no teeth.
Inverkeilor incontinent.
Coupar Angus barely living.
Longforgan – anyone know about Longforgan?

It starts to feels oddly like a wedding. Some banners are adorned. Pictures of the king and queen hung perhaps.

Music starts to play.

Macbeth and Lady Macbeth enter, in full ceremonial robe, giggling –

Macbeth
Whoa –

Lady Macbeth
My lord the king.

Macbeth
And my lady queen.

They giggle again – start to dance.

Fucking king!
Where is everyone?

63

Lady Macbeth
Out there, waiting for us to start the dinner –

Macbeth
It begins?

Lady Macbeth
Yes. So it does –

They take a deep breath, are about to open the doors.

The servant interrupts them.

Servant
A note came for your highness.

Lady Macbeth
Now?

The servant passes it to Macbeth.

Macbeth reads it.

He passes it to Lady Macbeth.

She looks reads it then looks at him.

So quickly?

Macbeth
So it seems. Efficient.
In a ditch with twenty bullets in his head.

Lady Macbeth
And Fleance?

*Lady Macduff, Lennox, Ross, etc., come in with balloons.
Pop streamers. Woohoo – a party!*

Macbeth
Fucking hell.

Ross
Good lord, give the cheer.

Lennox

Aye then we can drink with the king!

Macbeth

I will, come in, come in –
Fill your glasses.

Lady Macbeth

Our most loyal, gracious guests –

Macbeth

And with a goblet in all our hands, it is not to me but to
you I will raise my glass –

Lennox

Oh he's got a speech –

Lady Macduff

Of course he has!

Macbeth

My noble kinsman, you're the rock on which I will rebuild
the state; each and every one of you the soil on which I will
plant the seeds of hope, and your spirit the fire with which
we will charge ourselves. To you all and to Scotland!

They raise a glass.

All

To Scotland!

Ross

And our king!

All

Our king!

Macbeth

And our queen!

All

And queen!

Lady Macbeth
And to our stomachs – good digestion wait upon appetite and health on both.

Lennox
May it please your highness.

Macbeth
Here we would have our honour completed were the graced person of Banquo present – who I may challenge for unkindness rather than pity for mischance.

Lennox
Where is Banquo?

Lady Macduff
Riding.

Lennox
What, this evening?

Ross
His absence, sir, lays blame upon his promise. Please't your highness to grace us with your royal company.

Macbeth
The place is full.

Lennox
Here is a spot reserved, sir.

Macbeth
Where?

Ross
Here.

Macbeth
Which of you have done this?

Ross
What, my good sir?

Macbeth

Wait – you cannot say I did it: never shake thy gory locks at me.

Lennox

Gentlemen, his highness is not well.

Lady Macbeth

Stay, worthy friends, my lord is often like this and has been since his youth. Pray stay where you are – the fit is momentary. If you take much notice you shall offend him, and perhaps shall make it worse. Drink, and regard him not.

Lady Macbeth takes Macbeth aside.

Are you a man?

Macbeth

Aye, and a bold one, that dare look on that which might appal the devil – Banquo stands with us.

Lady Macbeth

Banquo is in a ditch, you had him killed.

Macbeth

Aye so they said, with twenty bullets in his head, but – see there –

Lady Macbeth

This is the very painting of your fear: this is the air-drawn dagger which you said led you to Duncan –

Macbeth

Why, what care I? If you can nod, then you can speak. If graveyards and tombs must send those that we bury back, then the stomachs of kites and vultures will be our monuments. And now he's gone.

Lady Macbeth

What? Quite unmanned in folly –

Macbeth turns to look again.

Macbeth

As I stand here, I saw him.

Lady Macbeth

My worthy lord, your noble friends do lack you.

Beat.

Macbeth

I do forget. Do not muse at me, my worthy friends, I have a strange infirmity, which is nothing to those that know me. Come, love and health to all, Montrose, forgive me, then I'll sit down. Give me some wine. I drink to the general job o' the whole table, and to our dear friend Banquo, who we miss – would he were here. To all, and him, we thirst and all to all.

Ross

Our duties and the pledge.

Macbeth see something again –

Macbeth

Get off – quit my sight! Let the earth hide you. Your bones are marrowless, blood is cold, you have no speculation from those eyes which you glare with.

Lady Macbeth has to speak to the room.

Lady Macbeth

Think of this, good peers, but as nothing but a thing of custom; 'tis no other, only it spoils the pleasure of the time.

Macbeth

What man dare, I dare. Approach me like the rugged Russian bear, or a tiger, take any shape but that and I shan't tremble – but.

Once again Macbeth comes to his senses.

Why, so being gone, I am a man again. Ha! Pray you, look here I am. Your glass is empty, let's have it filled.

Lady Macbeth
You have displaced the mirth, broke the good meeting
with most astonishing disorder.

Macbeth
How can you behold such sights and keep you the natural
ruby of your cheeks –

Ross
What sights, my lord – ?

Macbeth
There – that!

Lady Macbeth
I pray you, speak not; he grows worse and worse; question
enrages him. At once goodnight. Stand not upon the order
of your going but go at once.

Lennox
Goodnight and better health attend his majesty.

Lady Macbeth
A kind goodnight to all.

The thanes leave.

Lady Macduff comes and tries to intervene –

Lady Macduff
Do you want me to stay around, help you –

Lady Macbeth
No. Just go –

Lady Macduff leaves.

Lady Macbeth goes and puts a bit of tissue under the table.

She sits back down next to her husband.

The debris of the evening that wasn't is all around them.

Macbeth
It will have blood they say: blood will have blood. Stones
have been known to move, and trees to speak: augurs, and

things that are connected have by magpies and choughs
and rooks brought forth the the secret'st man of blood.

Lady Macbeth
No more.

Beat.

Macbeth
What is the night?

Lady Macbeth
Almost at odds with the morning, which is which.

Macbeth
I will tomorrow, and betimes I will, return to the weird
sisters, for now I need to know by the worst means, the
worst of what will happen. I am steeped so far in blood,
that going back is as hard as going on. Strange things
I have in my head – things that have to be done –

She looks at him.

He looks at her.

What?

Lady Macbeth
You lack the season of all natures, sleep.
Your strange self-abuse is the fear of the beginner only.
We are yet but young in deed.

She kisses him.

Sleep, sleep. You need sleep.

He leaves the stage.

She is left with the debris.

'Fucking hell,' she thinks.

Interval.

Act Two

ONE

The Carlin appears on stage and talks to the audience.

Carlin
Still here?
Eating an ice-cream! Very good. Glass of wine in your
hand? Excellent. The story's gruesome but why should
that stop your need to *consume*? Go on – stuff yourselves.
Finish your meal, don't mind me. Screw the sweety
wrappers into a ball why don't you and make as much
noise as you can. Or wait for the quiet bits – and cough.
Yes! No one minds. Cough loudly. Talk to your neighbour.
We'll just carry on. We'll just do what we always do – the
scene is set, after all. One king is dead and another now
on the throne – but you knew that part already, you all
studied it as children fresh out of the nursery.
The assistant doesn't like me talking to you, by the way.
He thinks that those on stage should stay on stage and in
their roles, and those out there – you – a whole universe
between me and you, whereas I –
I don't know what I see out there.
Tut tut tut.
Knock knock knock.
Rattle rattle –
This house.
Enough to drive you mad –

Lady Macbeth
Servant, where is my servant?

Servant
I'm here, my lady.

Lady Macbeth
I need to find those women.

Servant
What women?

Lady Macbeth
The three you said came to the gate.

Servant
I sent them away –

Lady Macbeth
I know, but where are they? We have to find them –

Servant
You told me to tell them to get off the land.

Lady Macbeth
He said he saw them on the heath so on the heath is where
we will start –

Servant
You're hurting me.

Lady Macbeth
I don't care if I am hurting you, we will find those women.
They are behind this. The scorpions in his mind are
because they put them there –

Lady Macduff appears in the mist.

Dearest – what are you doing?

Lady Macduff
Leaving, just for a day or so – you were occupied with
matters this morning and so I thought it best not to bother
you –

Lady Macbeth
What?
Why?

Lady Macduff
I choose not to stay here any longer.

Lady Macbeth
I don't know what could have happened for this
changeabout – we're sisters, are we not? If I was mad
before.

Lady Macduff
Cousins, as you always remind me, the root and tree of
our family are not as close as sisters.

Lady Macbeth
Cousins then, but close cousins, as children we did share a
bed.

Lady Macduff
Some time.

Lady Macbeth
Well where are you going –?
Do we not provide everything that you might want –?

Lady Macduff
The birds that were so vibrant are muted now – do you
hear? Where is the owl or the raven or even the starling –

Lady Macbeth
Oh I see.
You've heard some rumours, well so be it –
At least say it out loud.

Beat.

Lady Macduff
Say what?

Lady Macbeth
The reason you are leaving –

Lady Macduff
I'll say nothing.

Lady Macbeth slaps her.

Lady Macbeth
Say it.

Beat.

There is talk of treachery and you have heard it.

Lady Macduff
I take my leave of you: can that not be something that you grant?

Lady Macbeth slaps her again.

Lady Macbeth
If there are rumours and words against us, at least tell me from whence they come – which direction – tell me.

Lady Macduff
Banquo.

Lady Macbeth
Banquo?
Banquo's dead. He met his end upon his horse, did you not hear?

Lady Macduff
What? Banquo? No – he is in the castle.
I saw him just now – minutes ago.

Lady Macbeth
How can you have seen Banquo – you're mistaken.

Lady Macduff
He spoke to me as plain as you are now.

Lady Macbeth drops her.

What makes you start?

Lady Macbeth
I wish your horses swift, and sure of foot.
And so I do commend you to their backs. Farewell, Isobel.

Lady Macduff
Sister, farewell.

TWO

Lady Macbeth goes back to the castle. She looks through the house – looking for something.

Lady Macbeth
This isn't right, lord, where is my lord –
Those bloody men you commissioned to kill, they –

She finds Macbeth.

Why are you here? In this room.

Macbeth
I like it here.

Lady Macbeth
But – this very chamber?

Macbeth
This chamber has a charm, you said yourself.
The last king we had in this house, we put in this corner, did we not?

Lady Macbeth
Yes.

Macbeth
So now I like it that I sit where he did.

Lady Macbeth
We'll move the furniture out then, put in your desk.

Macbeth
No I like it as he saw it. The lavender has gone and the floor rinsed of his blood but –

Lady Macbeth
Dearest.

Macbeth
Get off me.

He breathes. Tries to get his composure back.

Macbeth has murdered sleep. Cawdor will sleep no more –
but kings they say slept well in this room.

Lady Macbeth
I'll call a doctor.

Macbeth
No doctors, there is nothing wrong with me. I am of
sound mind.

Lady Macbeth
The men who you commissioned to kill Banquo – where
did you find them –

Macbeth
They are trusty, I met them myself.

Lady Macbeth
I know, but thieves also, surely? 'Trusty' you say, but what
trust is there to ask a man to kill another? How could they
be honest?

Macbeth
They said they had with twenty bullets put him a ditch.

Lady Macbeth
Written words only? You agree – you never saw the body?
To trust them is – to trust a thief who tells you he has
made a jewel and yet never lets you see it –

Macbeth
Banquo is dead, I know that because his head hung low
with gore, and blood was down his cheek –

Lady Macbeth
But where is he now? If he haunts your every step – why
his silence this morning –

Macbeth looks around.

Macbeth
Banquo?

Lady Macbeth
Wake up please.
Dear one, I need you. The country needs you.

Macbeth
How can I wake when I am not asleep?

Lady Macbeth
Wake up.

Macbeth
I am awake.

Lady Macbeth
So where are these men now – these murderers?

Macbeth
I know not –

Lady Macbeth
In the marsh beyond the heath, the battlefield, where did you find them?

Macbeth
I know not!

He thumps her.

She looks at him.

You strangle me with questions. You fill up my nights. Was it this or that? Peace! This bloody business I will answer to you no more.

Lady Macbeth
Never touch me like that again.

Macbeth
I seek your pardon then. I know not myself.

Beat.

Lady Macbeth
Screw your courage to the sticking place.

Macbeth

But for what? Where is this new time? This new Scotland?
The men in the chamber that should be cavorting with me
and asking me for favour? They hardly dare to come
near – there are no petitions, no honest askings, no quiet
words in my ear. They run. And why shouldn't they? See
what I see.

Lady Macbeth

Your mind is fevered.

Macbeth

No, or if I am then this disease is also on you. It must be
fevered for there is no sanity else in what we have
started – or worse perhaps you haven't the fever yet and
are the more ill without it –

She takes his hands and kisses them.

I wish I had not seen those strange sisters.
I wish I had not told you.

Lady Macbeth

This is not a supernatural soliciting, this is fear –

Macbeth

Presently it will start with you.

Lady Macbeth

I know these women. Sir.
I have seen them.
The three that you saw, so fantastical you thought, I have
supplied and spoken with this last year and before.

Macbeth

You agreed they knew the future?

Lady Macbeth

No I only said that they said that –
Listen to me – all winter they chap at the gate and ask for
supplies and I answer them when I can but these past
months I answered them not – a mistake, perhaps, but

I do not like to supply these weird woman and so I think
they gather up the matter and turn to you – but this is not
a supernatural soliciting – this is natural in its making.

Macbeth
You seized upon their message.

Lady Macbeth
Yes.
I seized upon it yes and again I would, for killing Duncan
was our chance – but did I believe it came from beyond?
No. I thought they played with you perhaps and I saw
your belief –

Macbeth
You played with me too?

Beat.

Macbeth looks at her.

Why do they have a quarrel with you?

Beat.

Lady Macbeth
I saw them for a little remedy.

Macbeth
What remedy?

Lady Macbeth
Before I was delivered of our fifth child.

He closes his eyes.

Macbeth
I told you –

Lady Macbeth
I know, but – the fifth child in a line, all before gone to
heaven? What harm is there in a little medicine, I thought.

Macbeth
You trammelled with hell then.

Lady Macbeth
There is no hell.
It was a foolish thing perhaps yes – and when that child
also died I didn't like it that they still asked for pay.

Macbeth
You asked me where Banquo had got to – look down in
the ground.
I see him there –

She looks to the window.

Lady Macbeth
Where?

Macbeth
He walks by the yew.

Lady Macbeth
How can you see anyone at this distance, that could be –

Macbeth
The sun is again behind a cloud and he comes for me.
How long I can run, how long in this castle can I can
hide –

Lady Macbeth
You are king, my lord, please –

Macbeth looks at her.

Macbeth
But not the man you wanted.

Lady Macbeth
So wrong, every bit the man I wanted.

Beat.

He kisses her.

Macbeth
I need to sleep.

Lady Macbeth
And you will.

Lady Macbeth comes towards him.

Let me solve this. Banquo lives. And plays with you. I'll
get you proof.

He nods.

She holds him for a moment.

THREE

Lady Macbeth with the murderers. In an alley.

Lady Macbeth
Ay in the catalogue you go for men.
As hounds and greyhounds, mongrels, spaniels, curs,
water-rugs and demi-wolves are clept all by the name of
dogs. Thieves, you told my lord that you had killed him
and yet he lives, answer me – but to this I answer you –
how comest it he walks around my house? Do murdered
men walk? You did not kill him is the only explanation.
I will sign a million things today and your death warrants
will be the first unless you tell me that you botched it up
but will do it now –

Beat.

What, nothing? Not a word from either of you – to my
dungeon you will go. And your wives I will catch and your
babies I will boil.
Banquo lives, I know he does.
And you know it too –

*She notices that there is some blood on her hand. And
another spot on her dress.*

She goes to the servant.

Who put this there?

She looks down at her dress, tries to wipe it. It gets worse.

She takes the dress off.

Servant
I don't know, madam.

Lady Macbeth
It's dirty – I'll have another – is there another I can have,
call the assistant –

Servant
The assistant is busy.

Lady Macbeth
Call the assistants' assistant. I won't have a dirty dress.
Stage manager, technician, anyone backstage –

A new dress is brought for her.

Thank you.

As she is stepping into it, Ross and Lennox catch her.

Ross
The thanes are meeting south near Edinburgh today,
madam.

Lady Macbeth
They can't, the king is here.

Ross
They say they'll meet without him –

Lady Macbeth
That's not possible.
It is the king's council so –

Ross
I am just passing on what I heard.

Lady Macbeth
From whom?

Lennox
We have friends who are there.

Lady Macbeth
What friends?

Lennox
Menteith.

Lady Macbeth
Not a friend.

Ross
Kinross.

Lady Macbeth
Likewise.

Lennox
Montrose, Kincardine.

Lady Macbeth
No –

Ross
Birse.

Lennox
Cowie, Macduff.

Lady Macbeth
Macduff is there?

Lennox
They are all there –

Lady Macbeth
Well, if Macduff is there, we have nothing to fear. He is practically my brother. We'll get the king dressed and get him there, they cannot meet without him.

Lennox
No one has seen the king since the coronation.

Lady Macbeth
The king has been busy –

Lennox
There is a rumour he is fragmenting.

Lady Macbeth
The king has never been better.

Lennox
Then where is he?

Lady Macbeth
He is tired after his exertions; he will be well tomorrow.
You'll see – tomorrow he will be in fine form. Leave me.

Lady Macbeth goes to the servant.

Have you found those weird women yet?

Servant
Yes.

Lady Macbeth
And?

*As Lady Macbeth is waiting for the answer she is turned
around –*

Missy
Demand Macbeth.

Lady Macbeth
What?

Carlin
Be bloody, bold, and resolute, for none of woman born
shall harm Macbeth.

Lady Macbeth
For thy good caution, thanks but not needed –

Missy
Beware Macduff –

Lady Macbeth
Where are you?

Mae
We're right in front of you –

Lady Macbeth
I can't see you.

All
Demand Macbeth –

Missy
We'll answer.

Lady Macbeth
I am not Macbeth –

Carlin
Why find us then?

Lady Macbeth
To call you off only, this is not the scene –

Carlin
Macbeth!

Missy
Macbeth!

Mae
Macbeth!

Lady Macbeth
Stop it, this pyrotechnic – you must cease this spectacle –
Is this the best you can offer – but stop –

Lady Macbeth gets her shit together – manages to get away.

This is not the scene – ASSISTANT!

She takes a chair.

We meet in the village. In a café. It's cold outside, and I find
a space out of the wind and out of where we might be

seen – you sit down and I sit with you. I know you well and witches you are not. You are women, ordinary women. You blackmailed me for money after I came to you for help, and when I stopped paying you, my favour you didn't find, and when the winter was harsh – I admit I did not think of you or your child – I got you thrown off the land. I told the keeper of the fees that you could not pay and I told the factor, for that I can make amends, and will if you will come tell my husband this was for reasons natural –

They put something around her eyes.

They spin her around. She falls on to the floor.

Alright, if you insist on being filthy hags! Ugh. Is that what you want – ?

Missy
Show! show!
Show!

Lady Macbeth
Get this off me –
Why do you show me this?
No, I don't want to see. I won't look.

She holds on to the cloth –

She tries to take it off, she struggles.

She can't get it off –

We watch her see something in the cloth.

She buckles.

Eventually it ends and she takes it off.

She looks like she might be sick.

You know I will never accept that.
I will never *ever* accept that.

FOUR

The Doctor is talking to Lady Macbeth.

Doctor
It is an accustomed action with him. I have known him continue in this a quarter of an hour.

Lady Macbeth
What means it?

Doctor
This disease is beyond my practice: yet I have known those which have walked in their sleep who have died holily in their beds. How oft is it that he walks?

Lady Macbeth
Every night – he rises from his bed, throws his nightgown upon him, unlocks his closet, and look – observe him, stand close.

Doctor
Look how he rubs his hands.

Lady Macbeth
Again and again –

Doctor
A great perturbation in nature, to receive at once the benefit of sleep and do the effects of watching. In this slumbery agitation, what, at any time, have you heard him say?

Lady Macbeth
Nothing that carries meaning –

Macbeth wanders across the stage – trying to clean blood from his clothes and hands.

You see his eyes are open.

Doctor
Aye but their sense shut.

Macbeth

Yet here's a spot.

Out damned spot, out I say. One: two, why then 'tis time to do it. Hell is murky, fie my lord, fie, a soldier and afeared? What need we fear?

Lady Macbeth

Can you not cure of him that?

Doctor

Cure a mind so diseased?

Macbeth

What, will these hands ne'er be clean? No more of that, my lord, no more o' that. You mar all with this starting –

Lady Macbeth

Aye can you not minister to him, with a tablet or some such pluck from the memory a rooted sorrow, raze out the written troubles of the brain – there must be a remedy –

Doctor

Therein the patient must minister to himself.

Lady Macbeth

Throw physic to the dogs then. I'll none of it.

Macbeth

Here's the smell of blood still. All the perfumes of Arabia will not sweeten this little hand, oh oh oh.

She crawls over and tries to wake him.

Lady Macbeth

This is madness, lord, do not give yourself to this madness –

Macbeth

There's knocking at the gate: come, come, come come give me your hand. What's done cannot be undone –

Lady Macbeth

Stop, my lord.

Macbeth
To bed to bed.

He seems to look straight past her.

Get off me.

Lady Macbeth
No, you – stop.

Macbeth
I had a friend he met his end.

Lady Macbeth
There was no end – my love –

Macbeth
No more of that my lord, no more of that, you mar all
with this starting – I know I know, I'm clean I'm clean –

He is about to wander off, then comes back to her.

Cheer up, dearest chuck –

Lady Macbeth
I miss you, please –
Come back –

*He looks back at her with eyes that don't seem to recognise
her.*

Macbeth
And here's the smell of blood again and again –

Once again, he is lost to his own madness.

Lady Macbeth lets him go.

She stands and thinks.

She sends the Doctor away.

Lady Macbeth
Let him go his way unmolested this night, look after him.

She takes a chair and sits on it.

In truth keep him in the back chamber if that is where he
is happy.
Out of sight from anyone until his fairer temperament
returns. And he will return. In no time.
And bring me his desk.
All the business that was due the king. Foreign levies,
domestic dispute, dispatches –

The servant nods.

And –

A desk is brought.

*It's not exactly put in front of the chair, which is a bit
irritating, but she moves the chair so it's by the desk.*

Good.

She sits at it.

The servant nods.

And envelopes and all the reports and papers that were
sent for his reading I will do for him.

The servant nods.

And letters, anything that he has decreed, or that the
thanes would want him to read, anything that needs our
attention – the audit perhaps, the council meetings –
I need it all.

*The servant brings in the writing box and puts it down on
the desk.*

The servant knocks on it.

Why do that?

Servant
Just to check that it is firm and fixed, m'lady.

Lady Macbeth
I do not like it that you knock –

Servant

It's just a little knocking –

Lady Macbeth

I don't like it.

Servant

You've never said before –

Lady Macbeth

I have never liked knocking. This castle – the draughts around here mean that there is always a knocking, whether doors or windows –

Servant

Madam.

Lady Macbeth

You see now there is knocking. You knock and now there is knocking. Go and check all the windows and doors that they might be firm.

Lady Macbeth is at the desk.

She picks up the papers so that she might read them.

And some water, wine – I will be here all night – the place has been left with so much undone – if the notations speak true then Duncan left the country as a pauper and we would be wise to find a remedy –

The servant goes.

She reads again.

She hears a knocking.

She makes sure that it isn't the desk, puts a bit of paper under it.

She reads again.

Why is it always the English, the English, always the English.

She picks it up, she reads again.

Lennox

Something came out of the council meeting.

Lady Macbeth

It doesn't matter – it was a council meeting that the king wasn't at, so –

Lennox

They passed a decree.

Lady Macbeth

The decree means nothing, without him there –

Lennox

They do not accept that he is the king.

Lady Macbeth

Who does not accept that he is king?
Menteith?
Of course Menteith.
And Kinross, Montrose, Kincardine, Birse, Cowie.

Lennox

Macduff.

Lady Macbeth

No, not Macduff.

Lennox

Yes, Macduff.

Lady Macbeth

Macduff loves us.

Lennox

Macduff is headed south talking of raising an army.

Lady Macbeth

I don't believe it.

Lennox

His castle is said to the be the place where the spies do meet.

Lady Macbeth
He is not in his castle, I know he is not in his castle.
I know he is not in his castle in Fife because all this paper
tells me he is at the border, and now in England – can the
same man be in three places at once? No, I think not even
Macduff can perform a trick such as that.

FIVE

*Lady Macbeth goes down to the dungeons where the two
murderers are being held.*

She gets them out of their chains.

Lady Macbeth
Oh don't cry so hard, I could have had you in a rack.
A job I have for you – prove your allegiance.

She gives them a list of names.

Murderer 2
Montrose, Kincardine, Birse, Cowie.

Lady Macbeth
Yes. And Arbuthnott. Fettercairn.

Murderer 2
So many?

Lady Macbeth
Do it quickly. And silently.

She gives them pistols.

And another job, only more gentle in nature.
Go to the Macduff castle and bring the lady to me. Do
that first, do not go after her lord.

Murderer 1
And if she does not want to come?

Lady Macbeth
She will not want to come, of course, why would she want to come – but I am her sister. She is safest with me.

Beat.

I don't care whether you bring her in a sack or with her hands tied behind her back. But bring her.

Murderer 1 accept his orders and leaves. Murderer 2 stays behind.

Murderer 2
Good job, sirrah.

Lady Macbeth
I am not your sirrah, I am your queen. Do not use 'sirrah' when you see a woman. I think I am done.

Murderer 2
There is something else –

Lady Macbeth
Then say it quickly.

Murderer 2
I did not see Banquo dead. Not with these eyes. He had a light and we heard his voice but after we –

Lady Macbeth
Whoa. You did not see him dead?

Murderer 2
I did not, no.

Beat.

Lady Macbeth
Thank you.
And you are right, I will pay you more if you will write it down. Banquo lives and is still at large, I know it.
And Fleance perhaps.

Murderer 2

No, Fleance we killed.

Murderer 2 leaves.

She puts out the chair.

A bit of blood comes off it on to her hand.

She gets a towel and wipes it. Fucking hell: more. She manages to contain it.

Gets a few more chairs.

Lady Macbeth

How come this place is not clean? Assistant –

Servant

I am the servant.

Lady Macbeth

Servant. I meant servant.

Servant

I cleaned it this morning, I swept.

Lady Macbeth

Well, another sweep it seems to require – and these chairs.

Servant

Yes, with my own cloth I washed them.

Lady Macbeth

Wash them again and tell those within the castle to come in – Lennox and Ross are loyal I believe, and we have thanes and lords.

Servant

Madam I will.

Lady Macbeth takes a breath, looks around.

SIX

Lady Macbeth and Lady Macduff meet in half-light.

Lady Macduff
So you bring me now by force?

Lady Macbeth
Would you have come otherwise?

Lady Macduff
Do you know what they say about you?

Lady Macbeth
And what do you say back?

Lady Macduff
I don't like to believe it.

Lady Macbeth
Then don't.
You know who I am, and who I have always been to you.
This is a tricky time I will admit, but will come good by
degrees. A few weeks of this turmoil, and then the king –

Beat.

Lady Macbeth gets her composure together.

I didn't know you were delivered.

Lady Macduff
As you see.

Lady Macbeth
How was it?

Lady Macduff
You know yourself.
Hell.

Lady Macbeth
Yes, hell. And now?

Lady Macduff
Sore breasts.
The child doesn't sleep much. He tires me.

Lady Macbeth
A boy?

Lady Macduff nods.

Lady Macbeth comes over to her.

I thought you might have brought him – ?

Lady Macduff
Here?

Lady Macbeth
I thought you might let me see him, yes.
The cot we have here stands empty.

Lady Macduff
I'm not coming back.

Lady Macbeth
Of course I'm not suggesting, but these weeks – do you
really want to be alone? Please, Isobel, this time – the
thanes are in upheaval again – the only safe place is here
with us.

Lady Macduff
I am married.
I belong to my husband, Macduff has promised to return,
he hasn't yet seen his son, so even if I –

Lady Macbeth
You understand what you say?

Lady Macduff
Yes.

Lady Macbeth
You are my sister.

Lady Macduff
We are cousins, you always said cousins.

Lady Macbeth
And what about the baby – ?

Lady Macduff
What about the baby?

Lady Macbeth
I can try to keep you safe, but the lords that are loyal they are saying that the Macduff castle is the centre of the rebellion –

Lady Macduff
The Macduff castle is my home. The Macduff castle is my castle, I am Macduff.

Lady Macbeth
You said you loathe him.

Lady Macduff
He is my husband.

Lady Macbeth
If you will not see sense, okay, stand by your husband but bring the child here, I will make sure it remains safe.

Lady Macduff
Bring my child to you?

Lady Macbeth
Yes why not?

Lady Macduff
And then?
Hear that he died in your arms like all of yours?

Beat.

Lady Macbeth looks at her sister.

Lady Macbeth
What did you say?

Lady Macduff
I said, hear that he died in your arms like all of yours.

Beat.

Lady Macbeth
Tell me, what does this baby look like anyway – ?

Lady Macduff
You'll never see him.

Lady Macbeth
He looks like Banquo I wager –

Lady Macduff
He looks like a baby.

Lady Macbeth
Does Macduff know he raises Banquo's kid?

Lady Macduff looks at her cousin.

Lady Macbeth looks back at her.

Isobel please? I can't help you if you don't come here.

The servants recite the thanes of Scotland.

Servants
Montrose. Kincardine. Birse, Cowie, Arbuthnott,
Fettercairn.

Lady Macduff
Goodbye sister.

SEVEN

Lady Macbeth goes and finds her husband.

He is lying on the bed.

She sits down next to him.

Lady Macbeth speaks to the Doctor.

Lady Macbeth
How long has he not slept for now?

Doctor
Two weeks.

Lady Macbeth
Without any time being still?

Doctor
So seems it. Sometimes he nods a little, and we hope surely this drought will break, but as soon as he is down he is up and walking –

She climbs on to the bed beside him.

Macbeth
The Thane of Fife he had a wife. And the wife she had a chook, the both they were across the land and up before the rook –

She holds him close.

Lady Macbeth
Shushh shush, don't say that.

Macbeth
All that we do, we do together?

Lady Macbeth
Yes we do.

Macbeth
I had a friend, he met his end.

Lady Macbeth
    I'm here, I've got you.

She rocks him.

    And for what it's worth, those women said none of
    woman born shall harm Macbeth, so – a few days more,
    then we're both safe.
    There is no going back.

The servants continue to recite the names of the thanes.

Servants
    Montrose, Kincardine, Birse, Cowie, Arbuthnott,
    Fettercairn, Kinnaber, Menmuir, Clova, Kinalty.

Lady Macduff stands alone, she talks as if to her baby.

Lady Macduff
    And what will you do now? How will you live? As birds
    do, Mother. What, with worms and flies? With what I get,
    I mean, and so do they. Poor bird, thou'dst never fear the
    net nor lime, the pitfall nor the gin. Why should I,
    Mother? Poor birds, they are not set for. My father is
    gone, for all your saying. Yes he is gone. How wilt thou do
    for a father? Nay, how will you do for a husband?
    Why I can buy me twenty at any market.
    Was my father a traitor, Mother?
    Ay that he was.
    What is a traitor?
    Why one that swears and lies, everyone that is a traitor
    must be hanged –

*As she has been talking, blood has appeared through her
dress.*

We hear the sound of a savage stabbing.

She looks down at her dress.

Montrose, Kincardine, Birse, Cowie, Arbuthnott,
Fettercairn, Kinnaber, Menmuir, Clova, Kinalty, Tannadice,
old Montrose . . .

The sounds of a stabbing continues.

Lady Macduff is covered in blood. She screams.

EIGHT

Lady Macbeth turns a light on.

Silence.

Then the sound of a bird.

Chairs are set out for a council meeting.

Lady Macbeth
Some water please.
I have been too long at this desk – and –
A little water.

She rubs her face again.

She rehearses what she will say.

Macbeth is safe. The castle is secure.
Some thousand good, well there we are.

Ross
But Macduff and the English mean to start a siege.

Lady Macbeth
I heard it but I think we are prepared. Macduff is at large.

Lennox
His castle is surprised but he lives.

Lady Macbeth
It is the wrong way around then – I heard he was murdered.

Ross
Not so, but his lady sadly mauled.

Lady Macbeth
Who ordered it so?

Ross
We do not know but –

Lady Macduff picks up her chair and makes a scraping noise.

It seems to echo very loudly.

Lady Macbeth composes herself.

Lady Macbeth
A sadness then. My sister gone but her husband still on our tail.

Lady Macduff reaches down and knocks.

Banquo walks on, also covered in blood, and sits next to Lady Macduff.

Ross
My lord.

Lady Macbeth manages to compose herself.

Lady Macbeth
You mean my lady, why call me not so?

Ross and Lennox look at each other briefly.

It matters not but I prefer my title –

Lennox
Of course, my lord.

Lady Macbeth
Lady – liege.
Queen, in fact.

Beat.

Ross
Where is the queen?

Lady Macbeth
The queen is here.

Ross

I heard the queen is not well.

Lady Macbeth

You heard wrong. The king is not well – just temporarily indisposed, the queen however stands in front of you.

Ross

Then it is not as I see it. I see the king.

Lady Macbeth

This is the queen, I am the queen.

Lennox

Little matter, let's take our places.

Lady Macbeth

Little matter to confuse me so, I think it is a large matter.

Lennox

Perhaps we should wait, his highness isn't well –

Lady Macbeth

I am well.
I am well, I am not his highness but I am well.
Alright, you want the king, I'll be the king. So now I am the king. Are you contented? Can I be it by saying so?
First item, how many have we loyal to our army –

Ross

Some thousands, sir.

Lady Macbeth

Hang out our banners on the outwards walls: the cry is still, 'They come.' Our castle's strength will laugh a siege to scorn. Here let them lie till famine and the ague eat them up.

Banquo bends down to knock on the floor.

Lennox

Well said.

The knocking is echoing around. Duncan walks on.

Lady Macbeth
We will fight them on every front – we have friends, don't
we? Call all around – Macbeth is king by rights, and that
by means or strength cannot be denied –

She goes over to Lady Macduff.

Were you not warned, did you not use your head, you are
stupid yes but to go back to the castle – thank me that
your baby was saved, I had it written so.

Ross
Are you talking to the room or to yourself, master?

Lady Macbeth
I . . .
Mistress.

She sees blood on her clothing –

Excuse me.

She goes over to the servant –

I thought we agreed, I was to have a clean dress.

Servant
You had a clean dress.

Lady Macbeth
This dress is not clean – look, see?

Servant
I see nothing.

Lady Macbeth
There is a mark, a blemish.
How can I lead the country if I am in a marked dress?
These men already cannot see me as a woman – their eyes
are so accustomed to the male form as leader, so more
important is it that I wear a dress that is clean.

Servant
I don't know if we have another dress –

Lady Macbeth
Find another.
Or some water then – here's a spot, and here another –
Do not muse at me, my worthy friends – just a moment
and I will return.

A new dress is brought.

You should thank me, not haunt me.

She takes off her dress and puts on the new one. She hears a knocking.

Who is it that knocks?

Lennox
No one, sir.

She goes and puts a bit of tissue under the table.

Lady Macbeth
The table then, the table wobbles.

Ross
Can we discuss what supplies we might have for our men –

Lady Macbeth
Yes we can – begin –

Ross
Glengowrie has said his barn and all the feed for his
animals –

She double checks that the table isn't what is making the noise, then she sits down in the new dress.

Lady Macbeth
But some thousand you say. Glengowrie is not enough
alone. That is good news of course but Crannach is the
best we have? The new Kinross, Findowie – where is
Kinclaven with his offers?
Why has the Macduff infant not been brought to me?

Beat.

I said why has the Macduff infant not been brought to me?

Ross
It was as you asked for it.

Lady Macbeth
I asked that it was brought to me, I would raise it.

Ross
No, both dead, laid together in the same box.

Lady Macbeth
That is not as I asked for it – he was to be ours – here our heir.

Lennox
Crannach and Dalmarnock are coming to our aid.

Lady Macbeth
Will you answer me –

Ross
When?

Lennox
When they can get here – it is our nearest supporters we call for now.

Lady Macbeth
That baby was supposed to be mine –

Ross
Fintry, and Strowan?

Lennox
Aye appease them with news of how –

Lady Macbeth
Will you not answer me! Answer me! He was to be mine –

They look at her.

Blood comes through the new dress.

She sees it.

She speaks across the room to the servant.

Is this a game you play? To bring me yet another dress
that is marked?
Is this the limit of your villainy? To see a woman in front
of you, you must tease and disrupt, not even call her by
the title but insist that she be something that she is not.
Lady Macbeth is not fragmenting – and I am not mad.
Mad you will not say the queen was. The king lost his
mind yes but the queen, she held it together and made it
work as women must when men fold as little children –
Why can you not see a queen before you?
Excuse me. Another dress – assistant!
I will keep changing my dress, and I will keep changing
my dress and I will keep changing my dress until there is a
clean one on my back – Send out more horses, skirr the
country round, hang those that talk of fear – I will see us
through this siege, you know I will – A little water cleans
the dress – I will run this country and I will run it well,
excuse me –

*She is standing there trying to get the blood out of the dress.
Washing at it and scrubbing –*

Another dress – keep talking, keep talking I can clean my
dress while we are talking – another dress –

The Doctor comes in – Ross watches Lady Macbeth.

Doctor

It is an accustomed action with her. I have known her
continue in this a quarter of an hour.

Ross

What means it?

Doctor

This disease is beyond my practice: yet I have known
those which have walked in their sleep who have died
holily in their beds.

Lady Macbeth
What? No –

Ross
Can you not cure her of that? Canst thou not minister to a mind diseased, pluck from the memory a rooted sorrow, raze out the written troubles of the brain?

Lady Macbeth
Now wait a minute –

Doctor
Therein the patient must minister to herself.

Ross
Throw physic to the dogs then. I'll none of it.

Lady Macbeth
Whoa.

Doctor
If she will let me take her to be sedated, she might do better –

Lady Macbeth
This is not the script –

Ross
As you wish, just cure her.

Lady Macbeth
Get off me, I do not need curing.

Doctor
See she snarls.

Lady Macbeth
What? Do not say I snarl when I merely defend myself, there is nothing wrong with me that needs this cure – We didn't rehearse this, get off me.

They put something between her teeth.

She is silenced though she continues to scream through the silencing.

They put her in a straitjacket.

Ross comes in and sits down.

Ross
She was a woman most confused, why even times we saw her not as a woman at all –

Doctor
I will make sure she is comfortable.

Ross
And the poor country, almost afraid to know itself. It cannot be called our mother, but our grave.

Doctor
The country needs a steady hand, sir.

Ross
Foul whisperings are abroad. Unnatural deeds do breed unnatural troubles.
Move the desk to by my chair. Who put it here?
Bring me the papers, and the pen.
Things will be fair and calm in Scotland once again.

NINE

Outside the castle. Macduff with Malcolm.

Macduff
The tyrant won't endure. 'Tis the main hope from where there is advantage to be given, many of those loyal have revolted and those left find their hearts are absent from this fight –

Malcolm
Cousin.

Malcolm

What wood is this before us?

Malcolm

The wood of Birnam.

Macduff

Let every soldier hew him down a bough and bear't before him; thereby shall we shadow the numbers of our host, and make discovery err in report of us.

Malcolm

Now?

Macduff

Yes now. For Scotland, this is our time –

Malcolm

With the English army behind us?

Macduff

We'll get our country back.
And you, you'll have to grow up. Stop being afeared.

Malcolm

Where are these branches?

Macduff

On the trees, you idiot. Where branches grow. Though God knows how you grew on the royal one.

Macduff pushes him forward and they go on.

TEN

The queen upstairs, still in a straitjacket.

No one comes.

She pulls against her ankle chains.

Lady Macbeth
I am not given to hysteria, everyone knows – it makes no sense that I would lose my mind –

The servant comes in, although now she looks more like the Carlin.

Carlin
Give her some tea, Missy.

Lady Macbeth
What Missy?

The Carlin knocks on the floor. Missy and Mae come in –

I knew it, you haven't been my servant for a while – none of you, but in the castle –

Carlin
Your prop.

Lady Macbeth
I need no prop.

Mae
Sent by the assistant.

Carlin
It is needed for the ending.

Lady Macbeth
What ending?

Mae
Already the wood of Birnam approaches now Dunsinane –

Lady Macbeth
This isn't the ending –

The servant presses it upon Lady Macbeth. It's a dagger.

Carlin
We just do the play.

Lady Macbeth
What if I said I knew of a final scene?

Carlin
This is the final scene – the wood marches, the king laments, the queen kills herself –

Lady Macbeth
No – there is a fragment, unfound until now.

Beat.

Missy
There is no other fragment –

Lady Macbeth
Please listen, in the final scene – the fragment.
The queen does not die.
She meets the weird sisters once more. Perhaps on the heath? She offers them money –

The Carlin laughs.

Missy laughs, Mae laughs.

Alright, to say I help you is too much –
She leaves the castle.
She finds the man who dug the grave for her sister and asks him to check –
No.
That is not what happens.

The women laugh again.

She does not ask about the child.
Stop that –
This is a new fragment, but it is not your new fragment –
you are confusing me, confounding me –

Missy

You said it was an unfound fragment.

Lady Macbeth

But even if I was given to remorse and grief what would
she fall down upon? For taking the options that a man
would? For living in a life and place that was so brutal
that power by any other means was impossible?
Pull the curtain, I won't repent for her.
If that is the final trick this evening then no show.

Carlin

Give her some tea, Missy.

Lady Macbeth

I don't want tea.

Beat.

They were right when they said the play is cursed,
I understand that now –
We've been stuck in these, played out these scenes for
hundreds of years and whoever plays this part –
As long as they want blood, and the madness of women,
we are here to give it to them, is that it?

The women drink their tea.

I know I don't kill myself.
Would never.
Can't ever.
I know it was him that was obsessed with sleep and not I.
I know I am not made of the mettle of other women.
Those things I know.

Carlin

Good.

Lady Macbeth

What do you mean, good?

The Carlin picks up the knife.

Carlin
You weren't the only one they got wrong.

Someone knocks.

Lady Macbeth
Why is there always knocking – ?

They knock again.

Who is it?

Missy
Macbeth.

Lady Macbeth
What?

Carlin
This is the final scene, the fragment.

Lady Macbeth
So you have seen it – what happens?

They untie her.

Carlin
That depends.
Knock knock knock, open locks.

Lady Macbeth
No, don't leave –

The three women have gone.

Macbeth comes in.

She rushes at him.

Lady Macbeth
Thank God, darling. I've have been in a nightmare. Come
here, let me put my hands on you –
God I am so relieved to see you and up – are you fully
yourself?

Macbeth

Yes but don't come too near –

Lady Macbeth

Come too near? I'll climb upon you, mount you if we had time, but listen – we are in danger, they think I am mad. Let me kiss you –

She climbs on top of him – he pushes her off.

Later then.

There are supplies in the basement if we can set up a siege –

Macbeth

Ross, he came and told me what had happened, it was as if I was waking from a nightmare –

Lady Macbeth

What do you mean?

Macbeth

They say you are a witch.

Lady Macbeth

I know, but they always say –

Macbeth

They say you poisoned my mind, everything I did was because you told me so.

Lady Macbeth

But you will tell them –

Macbeth

I haven't slept for nigh on twenty days, how can this be something natural?

Lady Macbeth

What have you done?

Macbeth

They ask me questions – when came your wife like this, how it is her children do not live?

Lady Macbeth
And you say?

Macbeth
You killed your sister –

Lady Macbeth
For you.
For you I killed my sister, yes.

Macbeth
And her child.

Lady Macbeth
For us.
You killed Duncan.

Macbeth
For you, for you I killed Duncan.

Lady Macbeth
Oh, so *I* would be king?
So when you heard the word 'crown', murder was not an idea that first came to you – it was me I see – Duncan you could have thought would die of natural causes, he was old enough – but no, you are bent on this cause to murder –

Macbeth
Which you encouraged.

Lady Macbeth
But the thought was yours first.

Macbeth
How many have been dead these past weeks?

Lady Macbeth
I have been trying to make us safe – you safe.

Macbeth
No one asked you to.

Lady Macbeth
Yes you did.
And Banquo? How fits Banquo to your notion of
witchcraft?

Macbeth
How comes it that all our children die?

Beat.

Lady Macbeth
What do you say to me?

Macbeth
How comes it that all our children die?

She laughs in shock.

She looks at him.

Lady Macbeth
So I am reduced to my infertility after all. Even by you.
I thought I loved you.

Macbeth
And I you.

Lady Macbeth
But not, it seems.
What is it you have agreed?

Macbeth
They want to burn you.
If I let them not they will burn us both. They have ten
thousand men out there – Macduff leads his army well –

Lady Macbeth
Neither of us will survive.

Macbeth
Yes but you will die first –

Lady Macbeth
You know the tyranny was not mine, but yours.
It was not for me but for you I made you strong. Wouldn't
I always have been mistress to your master?
First.
Say goodbye like a husband.

Macbeth
And not see the knife you have at your back?

He stops her hand with the knife.

They kiss.

They kiss again.

Lady Macbeth
We did love each other once –

They start to fight –

Macbeth
No one can harm me, none of woman born, you told me
yourself –

Lady Macbeth
You underestimate again.

They continue the fight.

No man perhaps but woman of woman born?

He gets his hands around her neck.

He gets the advantage and is about to kill her.

Macbeth
Where is my underestimation now? We both know how to
murder, your disadvantage is that you got others to do it
for you –

A bird cries –

He looks up.

Cawdor –

She grabs the knife and slits his throat.

The bird is silent.

The room is silent.

She looks down at the body of her husband.

The blood pours out of him.

She gets her breath.

Lady Macbeth
He should have died hereafter.

She strokes his bloody face.

Tomorrow and tomorrow and tomorrow creeps in this petty pace from day to day to the last syllable of recorded time: and all our yesterdays have lighted fools the way to dusty death. Out, out brief candle.

She kisses him.

Life's but a walking shadow, a poor player that struts and frets his hour upon the stage and then is heard no more. It is a tale told by an idiot, full of sound and fury. Signifying nothing.

She cleans the knife.

I understand now why the assistant sent me this.

She holds up his head.

The tyrant. The tyranny, otherwise what I have known as love.
Curtain, fall now. This is the end of the fragment. Thank you, assistant, for the knife. We both die, of that there is no doubt, but don't let them see me killed also. Let them have the final image of this, the woman broken free of bonds –

Assistant, if it was you that hoped to change the tale –
assistant –
Drop the curtain.
Please – if you mean to change the story –

Macduff comes in.

Why is the curtain not falling?
A tale we have told, we have done our part – they still got
blood – curtain.

Macduff looks around, see Macbeth's body.

Macduff

Well, one is dead, the other soon –
Malcolm, wait out there –

Lady Macbeth

The curtain will fall, you do not get this scene.

Macduff

And there he is – the king.
Looks like he shat himself as he died.
In case you wondered.

Lady Macbeth

Assistant!

Macduff

Tell me how was it that my wife died?
Did she piss herself as the knife went in or – sorry, am
I frightening you? Or did she defy us all, and did her
mother perhaps tell her what mine told my sisters – if a
man comes towards you with a knife – fucking run.

He makes her jump.

Malcolm, I said wait out here – this is mine. Will you not
fight me then, hellcat? You're dead already – You won't
surprise me with your teeth and nails, the men below can't
wait to see a female devil, does she have three tits? A cunt
that is concave? Will they dig you out of your grave just to
fuck you again?

She looks frightened for the first time.

Lady Macbeth
Let them see me as I should be remembered – fearless, powerful and unrepentant –

Macduff
We will burn your body – and then I'll show it to my son.

Lady Macbeth
Your son? The baby lived –

Macduff
Yes, Lord Ross took him from the bloody scene and stowed him away –
Wait – what's this?

She turns her head away.

There are tears –

Lady Macbeth
No tears.

Macduff
You cry after all –? That's why you long for the dark –

She shuts her eyes.

He kills her.

He looks at her crumpled form. Beat.

You can come in now.

Malcolm comes in. Macduff sees him.

Hail, king, for that's what you are.
There lies the lady and the man. Both usurpers now are dead. The time is free. No more queens and kings of the devil. Hail, King of Scotland.

Malcolm
Me?

Macduff
Yes, you idiot. With me behind you.

He goes down on one knee.

Tidy your shirt up, you're King of Scotland.

ELEVEN

The heath, outside the castle.

Birdsong.

The Bloody Soldier sits picking his teeth.

Bloody Soldier
If we shadows have offended –

He thinks, tries to get it out.

If we shadows have offended . . .
If we shadow have offended, think but this and –

Lady Macbeth comes on covered in blood.

Lady Macbeth
Who's there?

She hears the birdsong.

She sees the Bloody Soldier.

I can't feel my feet.

Bloody Soldier
Aye.

Lady Macbeth
And my arms are all tingly.

Bloody Soldier
That's how it goes –

Beat.

Lady Macbeth
Have we met before?

Bloody Soldier
I know not, lady, but.

Lady Macbeth
I know not either, but this place – where are we?

He shrugs.

The heath?

Bloody Soldier
Perhaps.

Lady Macbeth
And this castle?

He looks up at the castle, he doesn't know.

I feel like perhaps I knew it once.

She looks around.

Bloody Soldier
They say there is yet a new king.

Lady Macbeth
What of the old one?

Bloody Soldier
His head is on the railings.
His wife's too.

Lady Macbeth
His wife?
Do I know her?

The Bloody Soldier shrugs again.

Bloody Soldier
Who knows?
All that is told about her is that she wept at the end –

Lady Macbeth
She wept?

Bloody Soldier
Aye she wept.

The other ghosts join them on the stage.

What's Done is Done

DAN REBELLATO

Alongside her original plays (but what is 'original'?), Zinnie Harris has, for approaching twenty years, been engaged in a stealthily radical campaign of creative, feminist intervention in the western dramatic canon. From her reworking of Strindberg's *Miss Julie* as *Julie* (2006) to *Macbeth* (*an undoing*) (2023) she has produced new versions of old plays that turn them inside out, recentring the women in these stories, bringing out latent meanings that seem to have escaped their authors, their critics or both. There was an historically displaced *A Doll's House* (2009), a mighty reworking of Aeschylus's *The Oresteia*, no less, as *This Restless House* (2016), a furious take on Ibsen in (*the fall of*) *The Master Builder* (2017), a powerful version of Ionesco's *Rhinoceros* (2017), and a brutally modern version of Webster's *The Duchess* (*of Malfi*) (2019).

And now *Macbeth* (*an undoing*). This is another daringly strong adaptation. Some of the most famous moments in all of world drama are removed, rewritten, replaced, speeches reassigned, characters enlarged, actions redirected. In Holinshed's *Chronicles*, one of the sources for Shakespeare's *Macbeth*, a king is murdered and the conspirators hide the body by diverting a small river, burying him under the riverbed, then restoring the original course so that 'no man could perceive that anie thing had been newlie digged there'.[1] Zinnie Harris has diverted the course of *Macbeth*, pulling it apart and reconstructing it – we might say 'undoing' it and re-'doing' it – such that Shakespeare's and Harris's plays are both wildly different and uncannily similar.

The women are closer to the centre of *Macbeth* (*an undoing*) than they are in Shakespeare's *Macbeth*. In the latter, Lady Macbeth is central to begin with, crucial to strengthening Macbeth's purpose, collaborating in the murder of Duncan, presiding over the first council of the thanes, covering up for her husband's panic at Banquo's ghost, but after Act 3 Scene 4, she disappears, reappearing briefly in 5.1, babbling in her sleep, only to die off stage shortly before 5.5. Lady Macbeth is from this play untimely ripped. It was once thought more becoming for women to fade into the background when the men are talking, like the executed Thane of Cawdor who was at his best when dying: 'Nothing in his life / Became him like the leaving it' (1.4.7–8).[2] Harris's Cawdor resists his forced exit, possibly returning as a bird that the men anxiously chase from the room.

These birds and these women will not be kept out. From the beginning the women are literally knocking at the edges of the play, demanding to be let in.[3] These women are also the stage managers, the illusionists, women with an eye to the critical and performance history of *Macbeth* ('The play is cursed I understand', observes Lady Macbeth). The women are turned away, but they return, demanding entrance. They are the guilty conscience of Shakespeare's play, like Lady Macbeth's sleepwalking nightmares. As Thomas De Quincey wrote in his famous essay 'On the Knocking of the Gate in Macbeth' (1823), it is the return of the outside into the interior of the play that brings out its horror.[4] And so it is here: eventually the walls are breached and our new Lady Macbeth grabs hold of the play, with all the implacable sanity that we see for the first half of Shakespeare's *Macbeth*, resisting the play and the critics' attempt to pathologise her, refusing to let her husband's guilty delusions tell the whole story – at least until the play has its revenges. In *Macbeth*, Lady Macduff is confined to a single scene (4.2). In *Macbeth* (*an undoing*), she has a different sort of confinement, being pregnant for much of the play, which gives her a far more physical, bodily motherhood (sore boobs and exhaustion, blood and breast milk) than the angelically doting mother of *Macbeth*.

In this, and so much else, Harris is drawing on the complexities and faultlines of *Macbeth*. True, some of Shakespeare's characters insist on neurotically traditional gender roles: Malcolm tells Macduff to 'Dispute it like a man' when his family is murdered (4.3.219) and as the mood turns murderously vengeful he exults absurdly, 'This time goes manly' (235). But, in spite of that, gender slips and slides: several characters fret or delight in being unmanly or unwomanly; the witches even have beards.

This is probably why there is a long tradition of pathologizing Lady Macbeth: Coleridge saw her as 'deluded by ambition [. . .] with a superhuman audacity of fancy'⁵ and for Charles and Mary Lamb, she was simply 'a bad, ambitious woman'.⁶ It always seems to me that in the play itself Macbeth greets the news of his wife's death rather ungenerously: 'She should have died hereafter' (5.5.17) feels perilously close to 'Blimey she does pick her moments . . .' Still now, powerful political wives – Cherie Blair, Hillary Clinton, Brigitte Macron – can be slapped down by being called Lady Macbeths. Harris's Lady will not have any of that: 'Mad you will not say the queen was. The king lost his mind yes but the queen, she held it together and made it work as women must when men fold as little children'. Both Lady Macbeths are renegades against the prisons of femininity and motherhood.

Macbeth is a play of blood; Shakespeare wrote more violent plays but in this one blood has seeped into the very texture of it: 'make thick my blood' (1.5.42), 'blood will have blood' (3.4.123), and the magnificently nasty 'who would have thought the old man to have had so much blood in him?' (5.1.33–4). Blood and other bodily fluids breach the boundaries of the body – and usually and regularly, women's bodies – just as the women breach the boundaries of the play.

The edges of *Macbeth* are dangerously open. For instance, it doesn't end and neither does it begin. The last speech of the play, Malcolm's first as King, is all about preparing to shore up his own power base, not the moment of serene regal benevolence we might expect. It says: it doesn't end here. Meanwhile, the first moment of the play brings us in at the end of something, 'When shall we three meet again?' being the Wyrd Sisterly equivalent of 'it just remains for us to agree the date of our next meeting'. *Macbeth* begins with an ending and ends with a beginning; as Zinnie Harris knows, it is a play of permeable boundaries and will remain open tomorrow and tomorrow and tomorrow.

This matters because *Macbeth* is obsessed with closure (would that 'this blow / Might be the be-all and the end-all here', 1.7.4–5). The word 'done' (or 'undone') appears more often in *Macbeth* – some 41 times – than in any of his other plays, despite it being one of Shakespeare's shortest. It is a sleek, driving play of action; it is a play of 'doing'. (It's the opposite of *Hamlet*, which perpetually defers and diverts action; here actions precipitate further actions, the second half of *Macbeth* an avalanche of action.) But in *Macbeth* every doing is an undoing, no deed is ever done, actions have no end, because to do is to be done for. It is a play where people are unseam'd, unsexed, unmanned, unmade.

Macbeth worries away at the ambiguities of 'done', one of those words that, like the witches, 'palter with us in a double sense' (5.7.50). 'If it were done when 'tis done, then 'twere well / It were done quickly' (1.7.1–2), says Macbeth drawing attention to the double meaning of 'done' as 'did something' and 'done' as in 'that's over'. The burden of his anxiety here is that we can never guarantee that, as Lady Macbeth says, 'what's done is done' (3.2.13). Early on, daring himself to act, Macbeth tells himself to turn a blind eye to his actions: let 'the eye wink at the hand – yet let that be / Which the eye fears, when it is done, to see' (1.4.53–4). There's an uncertainty in the tense: 'when it is done' can mean when it is happening (when it is being done) and when it has finished happening (when it is done with). 'Done' appears to be past and present, completed and continuous.

The meaning of action – of having 'done' – slips out of control. When Duncan asks Ross to tell Macbeth he wishes to appoint him Thane of Cawdor, Ross replies 'I'll see it done' (1.2.67) but, as we immediately discover, Cawdor is just the first of a series of elevations that will lead to murder after murder, because blood will have blood. A terrified Macbeth hears the bell that signals time to kill and he remarks: 'I go and it is done' (2.1.63), the last three words oscillating undecidably between 'I'll do it', 'I can't not do it', 'I'm done for', and more. The meanings start to double, double, causing toil and trouble. 'Done' accumulates increasingly murderous significance; of the 41 instances of 'done' almost three-quarters refer to murder and other crimes so that later, even apparently innocent uses of the word seem steeped in blood: 'may you see things well done there' (2.4.37), says Macduff to Ross about his departure to Scone and 'done' clangs in the sentence to make us doubt it. The sleepwalking Lady Macbeth, more in despair than expectation, tries to insist 'what's done cannot be undone' (5.1.65). But by now we know that the hurly-burly is never done and all doing is an undoing.

Macbeth (an undoing) sits in the ineliminable openness of *Macbeth*, its bodily openings, its incompleteness. It is one of *Macbeth*'s wayward children. Children form part of a famous critical debate over this play. In 1933, the British critic L.C. Knights delivered a waspish lecture entitled 'How Many Children Did Lady Macbeth Have?',[7] the title satirising the approach of critics like A. C. Bradley, who were popularly (and unfairly) thought to indulge in pointless speculation about fictional characters as if they were real people.[8] The puzzle arises from Lady Macbeth's declaration that 'I have given suck, and know / How tender 'tis to love the babe that milks me' (1.7.54–5) coupled with her husband's lament that he is childless (3.1.59–73).

If *Macbeth* does not textually resolve its puzzle, Knights says, then further speculation is pointless. Is he right? I'm not so sure: actors and directors (and writers, too) might usefully – and reasonably – use their imaginations to fill in the gaps. This argument would not impress Knights, who seems unwilling to acknowledge *Macbeth* as a play, drearily preferring to think of it as a 'dramatic poem'.[9] But this play is haunted by the terrifying power of the imagination and the images it summons up (daggers, birds, blood); to deny the power and value of imaginative sympathy would be out of keeping with it.

It is also packed with children: Banquo's son Fleance, the Macduffs' son, Duncan's grown-up children; the second and third apparitions in 4.1 are a 'bloody child' and a 'child, crowned'; Macbeth's downfall hinges on the nature of Macduff's birth and the play throngs with lines of children stretching into the future. (Harris's focus on Lady Macduff's pregnancy entirely responds to this texture in Shakespeare's play and in giving Lady Macbeth at least five lost children, Harris is knitting up the ravelled sleave of the play.)

The children proliferate metaphorically: Macbeth describes the duties he owes to the king as his children (1.4.26). Imagining the king's murder, though, he predicts it generating enormous pity, which he characterises as 'a naked new-born babe' (1.7.21). Later, resolving to act with greater urgency and immediacy, he says 'From this moment, / The very firstlings of my heart shall be / The firstlings of my hand' (4.1.161–3): 'firstlings' are one's first offspring and here the proliferation of children are an image connected with the disturbing proliferation of actions and their consequences. (Macbeth is wrong, of course: having children is never 'done'. Who gives birth to a child and thinks, well that's *that* done?) There are children everywhere; even the 'temple-haunting martlet' is said not merely to have made a nest but a 'procreant cradle' (1.6.4,8). In such a play, how can we not think of the children?

Macbeth, in other words, produces its own children. It is its own procreant cradle. It is a play of revision and adaptation: the original text (but what is 'original'?) seems itself to be a revision, probably undertaken in collaboration with Thomas Middleton. Soon after Restoration, William Davenant wrote a successful adaptation, which, like Harris's, has a lot more for Lady Macduff (though, unlike Harris's, underscores her traditional femininity to emphasise Lady Macbeth's gender-traitor villainy).[10] The play continues to be adapted, rewritten, responded to. *Macbeth* is never 'done' (and what play ever is?).

Canonical plays like *Macbeth* can feel like oppressive parents. To see the dramatic canon, like Banquo's children, as a long unbroken line of children-become-parents in orderly succession might overstate the case, but Zinnie Harris's incursions do seem Macbeth-like, in their resistance to the Father. (*Macbeth* is full of repudiations of parents from Lady Macduff's son talking sassily back to his mother [4.2] to Macduff's caesarean birth, which, as Janet Adelman argues, marks a symbolic separation from the maternal body that runs through the play.)[11] Perhaps we might think of the canon less as sheer parental succession, and more in the musical sense: an overlapping series of phrases that each echo the other, perhaps with variations of pitch, attack and feel, each only making sense in the context of the others. *Macbeth* (*an undoing*) makes its music in relation to *Macbeth*, but now, too, *Macbeth* makes its music alongside *Macbeth* (*an undoing*).

The nineteenth-century critic and playwright J. Comyns Carr wrote an interesting essay on Macbeth and Lady Macbeth, arguing that Lady Macbeth is haunted by the past and Macbeth by the future.[12] Carr was a man of his time and described these tendencies as natural features of the sexes, but it does seem to describe something valuable; it offers an intriguing vision of lines of history stretching back into the past and forward into the future, but fractured in the present by theatre and by gender. This feels like where *Macbeth* (*an undoing*) beautifully sits: an undoing that is also a doing.

January 2023

Notes

1. In: Geoffrey Bullough, ed., *Narrative and Dramatic Sources of Shakespeare, Volume VII: Major Tragedies, Hamlet, Othello, King Lear, Macbeth* (London: Routledge & Kegan Paul, 1973), p. 482.
2. All quotations from William Shakespeare, *Macbeth*, ed. Nicholas Brooke (World's Classics. Oxford: Oxford University Press, 1990).
3. Intriguingly like Hilde Wangel in Harris's/Ibsen's (*the fall of*) *The Master Builder*.
4. Thomas De Quincey, *On Murder*, ed. Robert Morrison (World's Classics. Oxford: Oxford University Press, 2006), pp. 6–7.

5. Samuel Taylor Coleridge, *Shakespearean Criticism*, ed. Thomas Middleton Raysor, 2 vols (Everyman's Library. London: Dent, 1960), Vol 1: p. 64.
6. Charles and Mary Lamb, *Tales from Shakespeare* [1807] (Everyman's Library. London: Dent, 1906), p. 143.
7. L. C. Knights, *Explorations: Essays in Criticism Mainly on the Literature of the Seventeenth Century* (London: Stewart, 1947), pp. 15–54.
8. In fact Bradley was very clear that 'whether Macbeth had children [. . .] is quite immaterial', *Shakespearean Tragedy: Lectures on Hamlet, Othello, King Lear, Macbeth* [1904] (London: Macmillan, 1962), p. 421. Despite this, Knights's attack was so successful that Bradley is widely believed to have written an essay with Knights's (satirical) title (see John Britton, 'A. C. Bradley and Those Children of Lady Macbeth,' *Shakespeare Quarterly* 12.3 (Summer 1961), 349–51).
9. Knights, op. cit., p. 18.
10. William Davenant, *Macbeth* [1674], in *Five Restoration Adaptations of Shakespeare*, ed. Christopher Spencer (Urbana, IL: University of Chicago Press, 1965), pp. 33–107.
11. Janet Adelman, 'Escaping the Matrix: The Construction of Masculinity in Macbeth and Coriolanus', in *Suffocating Mothers: Fantasies of Maternal Origin in Shakespeare's Plays, Hamlet to The Tempest* (London: Routledge, 1992), pp. 130–64.
12. J. Comyns Carr, *Macbeth and Lady Macbeth: An Essay* (London: Bickers, 1889), p. 24.